A Guide for Men Helping Female Partners Deal with Childhood Sexual Abuse

What About Me?

Grant Cameron

Published by Creative Bound Inc.
P.O. Box 424, Carp, Ontario, K0A 1L0
(613) 831-3641

ISBN 0-921165-38-2
Printed and bound in Canada

Book design by Wendelina O'Keefe

Canadian Cataloguing in Publication Data

Cameron, Grant, 1960-

What about me? : a guide for men helping female partners deal with childhood sexual abuse

2nd ed.
Includes bibliographical references
ISBN 0-921165-38-2

1. Adult child sexual abuse victims—Mental health.
2. Nurturing behavior. 3. Man-woman relationships.
I. Title.

RC569.5.A28C34 1995   616.85'8369   C95-900589-7

To my wife Liz, for choosing the right path

Foreword

I had one purpose in writing this book—to help the millions of men around this world who are doing their best to help adult female partners heal from the torment and trauma of childhood sexual abuse.

As the husband of a woman who was sexually abused as a child, I have a good, in-depth knowledge of what it is like to help someone deal with that horrid past. I know most of the traps and pitfalls, the things to watch out for, the goals to strive for. I know what it's like to see someone hurt. I know what it's like to see someone heal. Most of all, I have some good ideas about how you can get through it all.

There wasn't much information around when I began the long and arduous journey with my wife. A male who is trying to help a survivor heal is often left to his own devices with nowhere to turn for help. I compiled this book to help the men who aren't able to find the answers on their own. In no way does it take the place of a good counselor, but it will give you some insight on what to expect.

This book is for any male who suddenly finds himself thrust, without any guidance, into the dark, mysterious and problem-filled world of the adult survivor of childhood sexual abuse. It is for any male who has questions but can't find the answers.

On these pages, I draw on my personal experiences as a husband and supporter of someone who has gone through the painful process of healing. I talk openly about such subjects as sex and suicide, dreams, trust and anger. I try to educate, dispel some of the myths and misconceptions, and offer advice on coping and whether to stay or go.

Reading this book will give you a greater understanding of the issues surrounding childhood sexual abuse. It will help you to prepare for the rocky journey ahead. It will help you to understand why partners say and do certain things while they're healing. It will also help you gain a better understanding of your own actions and feelings.

Definitions
Some Common Terms

Partners of people who have been sexually abused as children are often thrust into the role of a supporter without any knowledge of the subject.

Some of the terms used when discussing the subject might be confusing to someone who has had no prior exposure to childhood sexual abuse. It can be downright confusing at times, and after a while everything sounds much the same.

So, to help you along on your journey, here are some common terms which are used in this book and which you might run across as you continue to help your partner through the process of her healing.

Incest is any sexual union or act between two people who are so closely related that their marriage would be considered illegal. For example, this would include immediate family as well as uncles and cousins of a child.

Molestation is any act in which an adult accosts, harasses or makes an improper sexual advance to a child. It includes inviting a child to perform a sexual act, attempting to force a child to perform a sexual act, or touching the child in a sexual manner.

Sexual Assault is any unwanted act of a sexual nature that is imposed on another person. Sexual assault can include touching private parts, kissing, fondling or any form of penetration. It is believed to be a crime of power and control, not an act of sexual passion.

Child Sexual Abuse is any incident of sexual contact between a child and an adult, regardless of whether or not the child agrees to it. This includes rape, fondling, exhibitionism, molestation and incest that takes place with or without force. Child sexual abuse should never be regarded as the victim's fault. The offender is always responsible for his actions.

What About Me?

Survivor is a female who has told somebody that she was sexually abused as a child and has chosen to actively deal with the past and get some help.

Supporter is a person who is willing and able to help a survivor through the healing process. The supporter could be a husband, boyfriend, relative or other person close to the survivor.

Perpetrator is the person who abused the survivor. They are most often male, they are usually known to the child and they are usually in a position of trust. Perpetrators may be the child's natural father, stepfather, uncle, brother, grandfather, neighbor, family friend or even a babysitter.

The Child Within is the entity or core ego inside the survivor which hasn't yet healed from the abuse. The child has a strong hold on the survivor and is responsible for many of her mood swings and anger stages.

Contents

Introduction

Don't feel alone, embarrassed or ashamed. Many men have been through it. We're all vulnerable, believe me. You could be a laborer, salesman, businessman or carpenter. It doesn't matter. It can sneak up on the most unsuspecting of us. One minute, you're fine. The next, it feels like you've been hit by a knockout punch. It hits you with a force you've never felt before.

If you're lucky and if you can find the inner strength, you'll be able to shake it off, find your legs and get up from the canvas to fight.

But your life will never be the same again, I can guarantee you that.

It happened to me several years ago. It seems like such a long time now, but it's a moment I'll never forget.

I was quite relaxed, sitting on the couch in my apartment, watching some television with Liz—who was my girlfriend at the time and is now my wife. We had been seeing each other steadily for quite some time, but I was just starting to get really comfortable around her.

At the time I hadn't thought much about it. But I'd noticed she was always a little distant. On a number of occasions—like the times I'd try to get close to her—she'd get really uptight and move away. At times, she'd just go very quiet and say nothing at all. Other times, she'd erupt like a volcano. I figured it was her personality.

That night, though, I learned that something else was bothering her—something that was deep inside her, something you couldn't see or touch, something she couldn't control, something which was ruining her life. As I sat there watching television, I noticed I was being studied. Liz was staring at me with a very strange look as though deep in thought.

11

What About Me?

Then, in an instant, she just blurted it out.

"I've been getting harassing phone calls," she said. "And I know who they're from—my stepfather."

"It's just one of the ways he tries to harass me," she added. "He sexually abused me when I was a young child and now he's still trying to control me."

There was a long period of silence as I searched for something intelligent to say. Here I was, suddenly presented with a very startling and unsettling revelation. Inside, I felt like a bomb had just exploded. But Liz kept staring at me, waiting for some type of reaction.

At first, I didn't know what to think. I was from a good upbringing and it hadn't entered my thoughts that such things happen in this world. I had lived a life sheltered from abuse. It was something I'd only read about—something I'd seen only on television or in the movies. I'd never really given the problem much thought. And never in my wildest dreams did I think it really happened to real people like her.

Questions began to flood my thoughts. I didn't know how to react. I sensed she was telling the truth, but I still found it hard to believe. Eventually—after several minutes of silence—I spoke up.

"What do you mean?" I said. "Why would your stepfather do such a thing?"

Liz paused for a moment, then went on to explain how her mother had caught him red-handed.

"So what's your mother going to do about it?" I asked. "What has she done about it? Is she going to the police? Is she going to leave him? Is she going to charge him?"

The questions came flooding out. It all seemed perfectly logical to me that something would be done. How could somebody stay with a guy like that?

Liz was a little evasive.

"Well," she said, "I don't really know. My mother said she'd handle it. He's done this sort of thing before, you know."

"What do you mean?" I asked.

"Well, he's always trying to harass me. One time he put pubic hairs in my toothbrush."

Suddenly I was enraged. How could somebody be so demented? How could a grown man do such a thing to his stepdaughter? What could I do to stop it? Why hasn't Liz done something about it? I turned to ask her.

At that moment, though, I could see Liz needed a listening ear and not a lecture. So for the next several hours she talked and I listened.

She told me about her childhood and how her stepfather sexually abused her. She told me how she'd wake up at night, to find him watching her with a strange, mad look on his face.

She told me how he'd ruin her clothes, embarrass her in front of her friends and family and, in later years, get jealous when she dated boys. She told me how he kept the family moving from house to house out of fear that one of the children would get close to neighbors and squeal on him.

She told me about the episodes in the bathtub, the attic, the times she tried to tell somebody about the abuse and how nobody listened or did anything about it.

She told me what had happened when she told her mother about the abuse, how her mother listened, then told the stepfather, and how later, when the stepfather cornered Liz alone, he called her a dirty little bitch for telling on him.

She told me about the sleepless nights, the nightmares, flashbacks and feelings of hatred towards men that she'd kept locked inside for years.

She told me of how the stepfather continued to harass her, how—in her older years—he still abused her, not physically any more, but emotionally.

As I sat there listening to this amazing yet sorry story, little did I realize that I had started on a long, arduous, rocky journey that would change my life forever. From that day on, I'd learn more about a strange and very distorted world—a world I didn't even know existed—the world of the survivor of childhood sexual abuse.

I use the term 'survivor' because any woman who has been through childhood sexual abuse, incest or molestation truly is a survivor in every sense of the word.

In this book, the word 'survivor' is used to refer to any woman who is healing from childhood sexual abuse—be it a wife, mate, lover or friend. I most often interchange the word 'wife' and 'survivor' merely because it fits more easily into the writing pattern. The term 'supporter' is used to refer to people like you—the person who is reading this book, the partner of the survivor, the one who is trying to help someone deal with the effects of childhood sexual abuse. A supporter can be any male partner—a husband, boyfriend or relative.

The 'perpetrator,' of course, is the person who committed the act of sexual abuse on the child.

In this book, I draw on my own personal experiences and those of others to try to answer some of the questions you may have about childhood sexual abuse, explain how it affects the survivor in her life and suggest what you can do to try and help her cope during this difficult period.

I don't profess to be an expert, but having first-hand knowledge, having gone through the ordeal, I feel my experiences will help you deal with some of the issues you may face as you help a survivor heal.

This book will give you some insight into the world of the survivor, why she feels certain things, why she says certain things and why she sometimes seems very strange when she's healing. This book will enlighten you about your feelings and how to deal with them.

You'll see, from reading this book, that there isn't much in this world of ours that can have such a devastating effect on a victim. There isn't much in this world that can cause such deep-rooted and long-lasting emotional problems in another human being.

The toll that child sexual abuse takes is staggering, from all accounts. The abuse steals innocence from a child and never gives it back. It takes away a child's security, replacing it with horrid, terrifying experiences, the memories of which will last a lifetime.

As you learn more about the roller-coaster world of the child abuse survivor and the effect it has had on their daily lives in terms of lost opportunities and mixed-up feelings, you'll begin to understand what I mean.

If you're reading this, chances are you have already taken a step on that long, rocky road to helping a survivor heal the dark wounds of her past. Chances are you already have experienced some of the pain and anguish that goes with the healing. Chances are you're already searching for some new clues and solutions to this emotionally charged puzzle. By now, you may be totally overwhelmed with all the emotions and problems encountered as a survivor begins to heal.

You're Not Alone

Well, I don't know if it's any consolation to you—but you're not alone. Millions of men around the world are in the same boat. More and more men are finding themselves in the delicate position of dealing with female partners who have been sexually abused as children.

Those survivors could be wives, girlfriends, co-workers or family members. In recent years, victims of child sexual abuse have begun coming out of the closet, in numbers far greater than we ever thought or imagined was possible. Women of all ages are now confronting and trying to heal the wounds of their past. They have been flocking to therapists, support groups, crisis and sexual assault centers, in numbers far greater than these can handle. They're newlyweds and young mothers. They're women who have raised families and only now are finding the time and energy to deal with the trauma of their past.

The problem is one that society has only recently started to come to grips with. But the statistics which have come to the forefront are overwhelming, to say the very least. They'll also make you sick.

Surveys of previous victims indicate:
- A girl born today has a one-in-four chance of being sexually abused before she reaches the age of 10.
- The average age of an abused child is 11, but it is not uncommon for children 3 years old or younger to be sexually abused by someone.

What About Me?

- This problem directly affects 75 to 95 per cent of all families.

The statistics are all very sobering—especially if you're from a good upbringing. So, when you're faced with the task of helping someone heal from childhood sexual abuse, there's a good chance you'll need help. As you go through this all-consuming process, you're going to need some way of understanding and dealing with this new world.

When Liz told me about the harassing phone calls, life as I knew it suddenly flew out the window. Like a gladiator to the lions, I was suddenly thrown into a life or death struggle, in unfamiliar territory, with no training at all and no books to help me cope.

I found out quickly that once you are part of this new world, it is very difficult, if not impossible, to turn back. The peaceful, happy place you once lived in is gone. In its place is a world full of problems, anguish, tough decisions and a seemingly endless number of challenges.

It's difficult to work through this process without some guidance.

That's what this book is all about—helping you to understand what the survivor is going through so you can help her on her journey.

Please keep in mind that the expressions, opinions and advice in this book are just that—expressions, opinions and advice based on my firsthand experiences with a survivor. They are intended to give you a better insight as to how you can best get through this healing process with a survivor. In no way can this book ever take the place of a good therapist or counselor. But it will help answer some of the questions you may have, enable you to work through some of the issues on your own and point you in the right direction by giving you the perspective of someone who has been there.

As the husband of someone who went through the lengthy and often tumultuous process of healing from childhood sexual abuse, I have a good understanding of some of the problems you might face and the questions you might have. I can't guarantee that the process will go smoothly if you read this book, but I can say it will make you more equipped to deal with problems as they arise.

There is little doubt that finding your way around in this strange new world can be a tough task. It can be painstaking and arduous, and at times it will test you to the limits. But, hopefully, with the help of this book, you'll stay on the right path.

Chapter One
Buckle Up

It's been a long day at work and you're looking forward to spending a quiet evening at home with your wife.

Things haven't been too good between the two of you lately. She's been moody—she gets upset easily and always wants to know where you've been.

Two nights ago, you'd had a real blowout and a lot of nasty things were said. She'd grabbed her things and threatened to leave forever. You'd convinced her to stay, but since then it hasn't been the same.

As you approach the front door of the house, your insides knot up and you silently wonder what today holds in store.

The drapes are drawn. The house is quiet. As you enter, you see she is lying on the sofa. The noise of you coming in wakes her. Immediately she springs to her feet. She appears angry, gives you a strange look, then snaps at you and quickly scurries up to her room.

You're left standing there, in disappointment and despair, wondering what you've done wrong. You feel alone, desperate, left out. The weight of the world is on your shoulders. You're in a daze, puzzling about what you said or did that could have upset her this time.

Well guys, take heart. My experience is that you probably didn't do anything wrong at all. It's very likely that what took place was totally out of your control. It could have been the shirt you were wearing. It could have been the look on your face. It could have been the way you woke her. It could have been the way the light was shining behind you. It could have been any number of things or nothing at all. Probably you were just the wrong person in the wrong place at the wrong time.

You see, you have just entered the dark and mysterious world of the adult survivor of childhood sexual abuse. You've become part of this strange, odd and upsetting new world without even knowing it. These types of mood swings, along with unprovoked fits of anger and rage, are very common among women who are trying to heal from the emotional trauma associated with child sexual abuse. They're just one of the many things that you'll have to learn how to deal with as the survivor begins to face up to the abuse of the past. It's not her fault and it's not yours. It's just something that happens.

I've had numerous experiences like this. I've walked in the door only to get lambasted for something, anything. At times during Liz's healing process, coming home was my biggest fear. I never knew what to expect. Sometimes she'd be in a great mood in the morning when I left, but when I came home at night she'd have completely changed. Eventually, I figured out it had nothing to do with me. I'd let her calm down then go and talk to her about the problem.

Liz says she would often get a sinking feeling when she heard me coming through the door. It reminded her a lot of her stepfather coming home from work. She knew I wasn't her stepfather but so much anger welled up inside her it was difficult to control. She didn't realize what the problem was until we got counseling. She began reminding herself that it wasn't her stepfather who was coming home, it was me. She eventually learned how to control her emotions and feelings and now she no longer gets agitated when I come home.

If you're the key person the survivor is going to rely on for support you'd better get used to this. And you'd better try to learn all you can about the subject of childhood sexual abuse and its ramifications very fast. The faster you learn about it, the better. Now that your partner is dealing with the past, you're going to have to be quick on your toes, really quick. You're going to need a crash course in something that the psychology books didn't tell you.

If your partner is already dealing with the trauma of the past, you can safely bet the ball won't stop rolling now. There's nothing you can do that will stop the process. And it's best not to try. So buckle up and get set for the ride of your life. It's not going to be easy and you're going to have to prepare yourself quickly. But understanding what she has to go through and learning how you can best help her through the healing process will help soften some of the blows.

With some guidance, confidence in the process and a bit of knowledge about what to expect, you can be a real asset in her successful recovery. Without it, though, you can be a real hindrance. After all, she needs all her energies to deal with the trauma of the past. The easier you make it for her, the quicker she'll get better.

It Isn't Easy

Helping the survivor stay on the right path isn't as easy as it sounds. It takes a lot of everything—patience, understanding, compassion and guts. Yes, plain old intestinal fortitude, because you'll be tested to the extreme. Your emotions will be taken from the highest highs to the lowest lows.

At times, you'll be distanced from the survivor. Then, she'll want you close. At times you'll argue with the survivor. Then she'll want your guidance. At times you'll laugh with her. Then she'll want your shoulder to cry on.

Sound complicated? Sound confusing? Well, it is. So, if you've decided to help someone deal with the trauma of childhood sexual abuse—whether it be a spouse, girlfriend, friend or family member—you need to develop a healthy appetite for more knowledge on the subject.

First and foremost, you should understand that the survivor is just that—a survivor. She never asked for something like this to happen. It found her.

She became a victim in one of the worst ways. What happened to her was a crime. She wasn't a consenting adult when the abuse took place. She was just an innocent child. She was a child who knew nothing about sex or sexuality. She just followed the orders of an adult.

Never blame the survivor for what happened. Her decision to

confront the past deserves a badge of courage, not a slap on the wrist. Remember, she was young and vulnerable and had no control over what happened. When she decides to confront the past, she needs your support, not your anger. Instead, the blame should be put squarely where it belongs—on the shoulders of the perpetrator. He's the only culprit here. He was probably someone much older than her, probably someone she really trusted, someone who knew what he was doing and knew it was a crime. The child who was abused was too young to know better.

In Liz's case, the assailant was her stepfather. He was much older than she and he was in a position of trust. He abused that trust and tricked her into performing indecent acts. He'd convince her she was doing the right thing. Afterwards, he would act as if nothing had happened. As Liz got older, he would psychologically abuse her by insulting her in front of boyfriends and calling her retarded.

Believe Her

It's very common for perpetrators to control children by using coercion or threats. In one reported case, a 7-year-old girl testified that her abusive father said her mother would die if the child revealed their sexual secrets.

"I felt scared," the girl told a jury in explaining why she didn't talk about her father's petting and intercourse. The girl also testified that she tried to phone someone to tell them about her situation, but her father stopped her by putting his hand over her mouth.

By now, I'm sure you realize why it's so very important to believe the survivor when she tells you she has been abused. There have been rare cases in which women have lied about the abuse. But that has usually occurred in cases which involved a child custody dispute where it served a purpose to concoct a lie. You may also have heard about a phenomenon called false memory syndrome. That occurs when a person gets brainwashed by a therapist into thinking abuse occurred when, in fact, it did not. But these cases are also rare.

In the vast majority of cases, women don't make up stories

about childhood sexual abuse. When your partner tells you she's been abused as a child, you can bet she's thought long and hard about it. After all, she's got nothing to gain and everything to lose by telling you, right?

Liz told me one of the toughest things about her healing was getting up the courage to tell me that she had been abused. It tore her apart. She spent many sleepless nights just trying to figure out a way to get it out in the open. She'd pluck up the courage only to back down. She even tried forgetting it ever happened, because she wasn't sure how I'd react. Eventually, though, the feelings became so strong she had to tell me. Afterwards, she said, she was relieved she'd told me. It was as if a weight had been lifted from her shoulders.

Admitting that the abuse occurred is one of the toughest, most gut-wrenching steps for the survivor because once the cat is out of the bag, there's no denying it. The survivor can't forget it. She can't just turn her back on it any more. Once the truth is out, there's no turning back. It's awfully hard to tell somebody something so personal and traumatic, then later deny that it ever happened. So, when the truth does come out, be assured she's not making it up. Be supportive.

Unfortunately, it doesn't always work out the way you'd like it to. The first time you hear of the abuse, it's natural to feel a little shell-shocked. After all, there's no nice way to learn some pervert molested your partner as a child. Suddenly, your whole life gets turned upside down. There's not much in this world that can stir up such revolting and repulsive thoughts as child sexual abuse, molestation or incest. It really tugs on your emotions.

I clearly remember when Liz told me she'd been sexually abused as a child. It blew my mind. All of a sudden I was faced with something I knew nothing about. I was at a loss for words. It took time to digest.

Truth Is Tough

No doubt about it—finding out the truth can be a real crusher. You may have lived with your partner for years, unsuspecting that something like sexual abuse had occurred in her childhood. When the ugly truth does come out, it hurts. So what do you do when confronted with it? Well, first wait until your head stops spinning, then take a deep breath and start thinking and listening. It's the only way you're going to fully understand what she's going through.

A lot of supporters get taken aback when they first hear of the abuse. When thoughts of childhood sexual abuse conjure up visually revolting images in our minds, it's very physically unsettling for a man. When we're confronted with it, a gnawing fear creeps in. We hear about it, read about it and see it on television, but it's always viewed at a distance. It's always somebody else's problem. When it's yours, it hits home.

I don't know if it's any comfort, but try to remember you're not alone in all this. Millions of men are going through the same thing. It takes a lot of supporters by surprise—even if they've known the survivor for quite a length of time. Don't be ashamed of your first reaction. Like most men, you probably didn't think much about it—until your partner told you it did happen. It's a natural reaction to clam up, pretend you didn't hear or just try to brush off the subject. It takes some time to digest this revelation.

In some cases, supporters refuse to even talk about it. Others ask the survivor to forget about the whole thing and leave it in the past. While these may be very natural first reactions for some people, they're also very wrong.

Eventually, you're going to have to face up to the harsh reality of the situation; you're going to have to come to grips with this and deal with it head on. There are no two ways about it. There's no way to brush something like this under the carpet; it just doesn't work that way. Sorry, but it doesn't. If you try, it's a sure bet that, sometime down the road, the dirt will come to the surface again. The sooner you learn to accept and deal with the abuse, the better off you are.

Before You Begin

Now this may all sound like a job for Superman—and perhaps it is—but unfortunately, in this world he doesn't exist, so you're going to have to handle this all by yourself, with the help of this book, of course.

However, before you begin there are a few things you should know. Every survivor can use a supporter—a trusting person who will share her pain and listen, but not judge her, when she has something to say.

That job often falls to the husband, friend or any male partner of the abused person. Problem is, few husbands and partners get any training in how to deal with this issue, not to mention all the trying little problems that crop up along the way. So, with little training and big lack of practical know-how, you find yourself thrust into a situation you have no control over, yet are expected to cope with. Now—with this massive load on your shoulders—you have to learn by the seat of your pants.

It's not surprising, then, that supporters have such a tough time with all this. It's also no surprise that supporters need help themselves.

I think the importance of the supporter has not yet been recognized by our society. While survivors usually have access to support groups and counseling services, the supporter is often left out in the miserable cold. There's just not a lot out there for the guys who painfully plod through the process with a survivor. Private therapists can be found, but they are often expensive and sometimes inexperienced in dealing with men in such sensitive predicaments.

I remember the tough time Liz and I had finding a good therapist. We went through the phone book searching for one, but when we phoned they were all very busy and dealt primarily with people who had marriage and family counseling problems. Eventually we got referred to a therapist by a friend. We stayed with that therapist for more than a year and she helped us tremendously.

Problems are also posed by the fact there hasn't been much written for men who find themselves in this type of situation. And most of what has been published is by therapists who haven't been through the process on a personal level.

So, if you're a male supporter looking for help, don't expect to find too much out there. The best thing you can do is pull yourself together and learn all you can about the subject of child abuse. You need to get hungry for information, you need to read this book and you need to get ready for some action. You can help by encouraging the survivor and giving her the time she needs to heal. It's a very time-consuming and tiring job. If the survivor wants professional assistance, you can also help her find a good counselor.

There are many counselors around, but the best way to find a good one is by word of mouth. Call a local sexual assault center or women's shelter in your community to find out who has a good reputation. If that doesn't work, try your local police station or hospital. They often have people who handle sexual assaults and are in contact with people who deal with these types of situations. Although police are not a social agency, my experience has been that they don't mind referring people who are in legitimate need of help.

Safeguard Yourself

Although it is your job to help the victim as best you can, don't get too caught up in the whole process yourself. Many supporters get overwhelmed by it all and aren't much of a help in the long run because they have too many of their own problems and feelings to deal with.

Sometimes I used to get so overwhelmed with all the problems, I felt as if my head was going to explode. It was really difficult to handle everything. When I couldn't cope any more, I scheduled a break for myself. Occasionally it meant taking a short vacation from work. Other times, it meant getting away with Liz to a cottage where we could relax. Being in a totally different environment really seemed to help. We left our problems behind while we were there.

You have a right to be concerned about the survivor as she goes through the healing process, but remember it's also a job she must complete on her own. You can't do it for her. She must make her way through each stage of healing in her own way. And for heaven's sake, don't feel guilty when she's doing this. It's not your fault that this happened to her. Remember, you weren't around to prevent the abuse, so don't feel it was your fault. Don't take on this added burden.

But that doesn't mean you can't help in her future. This is your responsibility; this is where you can really make a big difference. You're in a position to be a real support to the survivor. You can play a big part in her recovery.

In the following chapters I'll talk about some of the problems you can expect to encounter. I'll also give you advice on how to help the survivor in a crisis and answer some common questions asked by men helping a survivor. I'll talk about sex with the survivor, coping, anger and what to do if she talks about suicide.

Using some of the principles and information in this book, you'll be a support rather than a hindrance as the survivor begins to heal. You'll develop a greater understanding of what she is going through and learn the best way to effectively deal with her emotions.

If you have a working knowledge of the circumstances surrounding childhood sexual abuse and a greater insight into the problems it can cause, you can help the survivor set a goal and work with her to achieve it.

It might seem like a lot of work, and it is, but you can rest assured that in the end, when the survivor has completed her healing, she will be a better person. And so will you.

So let's get started. Buckle up and read on.

Points to Remember

- Don't blame your partner for what happened.
- The sooner you face the situation the better.
- The healing process isn't easy.
- Be prepared for mood swings.
- Find a good counselor.
- Don't get overwhelmed.

Chapter Two
Decision to Heal

Healing is not any easy process by any means. The truth is it's an extremely painful and difficult thing to go through, both for a survivor and for a supporter.

It can drain both of you, mentally as well as physically. It can disrupt your whole life and cause a myriad of unforeseen and difficult-to-solve problems. I remember waking up some mornings as though I'd never been to sleep. I would toss and turn all night, thinking about the day before, then I'd wake up in the morning too tired to face the day ahead. It catches up on you after a while. It can take its toll.

But healing from childhood sexual abuse is something that is necessary for the survivor—if she's ever to live a normal life, that is. It's something the survivor must go through if she's ever going to experience the true joy of living a life free from fear, anger and that ever-present demon, hatred.

Instead of dealing with the past, some survivors try to forget it ever happened. In some cases that can work—it depends a lot on the severity of the abuse, how often the abuse occurred and what age the survivor was when the abuse occurred, as well as what the rest of the survivor's upbringing was like.

Some women go through their entire lives without ever healing from the past. Others are well aware they have a problem but try to cover it up. Still others complain about it all the time, but never do anything to try to heal themselves.

Unfortunately, childhood sexual abuse always leaves its mark. For most survivors, the memories continue to haunt their everyday lives. It's easy to see why. A child who doesn't heal from the torture and trauma of sexual abuse lives in a world that is very different from the one most of us know.

An abused child who grows up without getting help for her problems faces a number of difficulties. You'll have to just try and do your best to understand this. Her values can be distorted. Trust is non-existent. Happiness is something only other people feel.

Psychological effects of abuse are often greater when the abuse has involved physical violence or if the child was abused by a trusted person. Brief periods of abuse usually have less of an impact than abuse which continues over a long period of time. Also, children who were abused when they were very young usually show fewer psychological effects than children who were abused when they were older.

The reactions of family members and others to the child telling that abuse has occurred can also have an impact. Calm, supportive reactions from family members can reduce the effects of abuse, but disorganized, disruptive, extreme responses can create further psychological problems for the child who was abused.

Here are some other factors which affect the impact of abuse on a child:

- the nature of the abuse
- he frequency and duration of the abuse
- the relationship between the child and the perpetrator
- the developmental level of the child
- the gender of the child and of the adult
- the age difference between the child and the perpetrator
- the rewards offered to the child

It gets very complicated, you see, by the fact that a child is not like an adult. When an adult is abused, the adult knows what is happening and the adult's emotions are usually developed enough to get through traumatic times. When a child is sexually abused, the child doesn't know whether it's right or wrong. The child may feel that what she's doing is wrong, but the child often gets a reward and praise for what she's doing so she becomes confused by it all.

I remember Liz telling me how she'd let her stepfather abuse her because she was so terrified that he would get angry with her if she tried to stop him. Although she felt it was wrong, she let the abuse continue because she was so afraid of what would happen.

What About Me?

She kept trying to convince herself it was okay. When the stepfather had finished abusing Liz, he rewarded her, confusing her even more as to what was right and wrong. Her body felt it was wrong, but her stepfather told her it was right.

The Child's Defense Mechanism

It's only natural for a child to feel confused when she is being sexually abused. The child feels so many different emotions and has trouble sorting them out. The child may feel anger, fear, shame and guilt.

When the abuse occurs, something very strange happens to the child. Because her emotions can't handle what's happening, a sort of self-defense mechanism kicks in. The child dissociates from the abuse. The child might shut off the normal emotions and instead focus on something else—something that can be a comfort while the abuse is taking place. The child may distance the mind from all the conflicting emotions that are surfacing. The child may listen to music that's playing, focus on something else in the room or just plain daydream. Somehow, though, the child's mind is on something else while the abuse takes place.

This emotional separation is the child's way of dealing with the abuse. As the child grows, all the hurt and anger that she didn't vent and deal with then plays havoc with her emotional development. She's left with a very distorted view of the world around her.

Liz used to tell me how she hated men. She didn't really have a good reason. It was just something that was inside her. Her favorite lines were "All men are the same" and "You're just like all the other men." The abuse had left her with a dysfunctional attitude towards men. She assumed that all men were the same as her abuser. She assumed they were all out to harm her. As she grew older, Liz still held onto the belief that men were bad. I've since talked to many other women who have been abused and found that most of them feel the same way. All the hurt and anger they didn't vent and deal with as a child is carried into the adult life of the survivor, and without proper therapy that's where the anger stays.

The Child Within

Sometimes all this abuse and the damage it did to the child leads to the development of another personality within the child. Sounds crazy, doesn't it? Sure it does, but the unfortunate part is it's true. We call this personality the child within, or the inner child.

It's something you're going to have to learn more about and it's something I've devoted an entire chapter to later on in this book. It's a concept that is strange, frightening and fascinating. It's something you can't see or touch, but it's real to the survivor.

The child within can best be described as a personality within a personality. It has its own thoughts and temperament. It has its own feelings and frustrations. It's like a little person living inside the adult survivor. The child within is really the entity or core ego that was abused and never healed from that abuse.

The child within has the same traits and personality as an abused child. The child within usually doesn't trust men or strangers and can erupt in fits of anger at a given moment. At times, she controls the adult and wants the adult to herself. She can be insatiable, never getting enough love and attention from the survivor. She can also be excessively needy.

As a supporter, you may have to take a step back and give the survivor some space and time so she can deal with this entity. If the survivor neglects the child within, the healing process may proceed at a much slower place or stall completely. It's very important for the survivor to take time out and help deal with the child's emotional wounds. When the child within is seeking attention, she needs and wants it right away. The child within is just like a baby—it won't rest until it gets the attention it demands.

Liz would often take time out to deal with the child within. She could always tell when the child was acting up because she'd have strange thoughts. She didn't actually talk out loud to the child—it was more like inner reflecting. If you asked her what the child within wanted, Liz would go silent for a bit, as though she was communicating through telepathy. Then, a few moments later, she'd respond to my question. She could actually picture the child, either sitting by herself or playing in a room. But try as she might, she could never see the child's face.

Yes, all this may sound rather strange, but it gives you some idea of how deep and complicated the healing process can be. It's good for you to have some knowledge of this so that you won't try to rush the survivor through her healing process. You don't have to fully understand the child within, but you should be fully aware it's there, it's real and she's not making it up.

By now, your head is likely spinning. You might be thinking that all this is too complicated, wacky or far out. You might be wondering what you've gotten yourself into and how you'll ever deal with it all. Well, breathe a sigh of relief. It's perfectly natural. It's also perfectly natural to feel overwhelmed at times. So, if you find yourself getting bamboozled by all this information at once, just put this book down and take a rest. Nobody said you had to learn everything overnight. It's better to learn a lot slowly than nothing fast.

Sure, it's important you stay one step ahead of the game. It's nice to know what could be around the corner. But don't forget you aren't any good to the survivor if you're a basket case yourself. If you find yourself getting too uptight and confused, simply put the book down and take a break. Then, when you're comfortable again, pick it up and go on reading.

Hopefully, by this point, however, you're convinced as to why it is so important for the survivor to heal. Hopefully, you also realize why it is so very important for the survivor to get really good professional help. If she doesn't, it can continue to affect her relationships, her attitudes and her behavior—all in a negative manner.

Recognizing the Signs

The abuse suffered as a child can surface in a number of ways as an adult. It can cause overeating, emotional problems, depression or abuse of alcohol and drugs. You've probably seen some telltale signs long before the survivor ever told you about the abuse she suffered as a child. You just didn't recognize it for what it was.

It may have been the time she walked out of the movie theater when a case of molestation was being played out on the screen in front of her. It may have been the time she got upset when you refused to take her for an ice-cream. It could have been the time she flew off the handle when you wanted to talk about starting a family.

These are all very common signs that somebody has been sexually abused as a child. Other signs are compulsive behaviors and an inability to trust or form friendships. It's quite common for women who've been abused as children to get into trouble with the law, become prostitutes or get into a life-or-death type of struggle within themselves.

Don't get me wrong here. This doesn't happen to all women who have been abused as children. This doesn't mean that all women who overeat have been abused. It doesn't mean that all women who get angry or throw a fit have been molested as youngsters. The point I'm trying to make is that the problem eventually does manifest itself in some way or another.

With Liz, I noticed it was her self-confidence and how she perceived her body. She was always worried about her weight. Although she is by no means heavy, she was always worried about getting fat. Her abuser was obese, so it followed that her inner conscience was worried about looking the same way. Even to this day, she worries about her weight. Her self-confidence is a lot better now, but she occasionally still doubts her abilities.

Three Stages

From my experience, there are three main stages in the healing process. They're the same three stages that anyone goes through when they suffer a significant loss. One is the crisis stage, another is the suffering stage and yet another is the resolution stage.

Now, this might seem a rather simplistic approach to some, and it probably is, but these are the three main stages which I witnessed as Liz was healing. This is also the order in which I witnessed them. Some experts in the area of childhood sexual abuse suggest the crisis stage does not always come before the

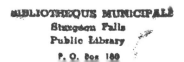

suffering stage and I have no reason to dispute that. They also say not everyone goes through all three stages. I have no reason to dispute that either. I merely want to give you some insight into what to expect during each stage, based on the experiences I had, in hopes that it might make you better prepared to help the survivor through it.

I found that the stages overlap, meaning the survivor might move on to another stage only to return to a previous stage to take care of some healing she may have missed. It can be a very frustrating experience to see the survivor regress to a previous stage, just when you thought she was past it. But don't get too frazzled when this happens. She probably just missed something and had to go back to work it out. It's better she do it now rather than later.

Before we move on, I want you to understand that the healing process is a very complicated and difficult thing. I don't want to leave you with the impression it's not. The information I present in this book should not be taken as the gospel truth. In fact, I'd encourage you to read other material and find out what others have to say about the healing process. The more information you have, the better off you are. Each case, each person, each relationship, each survivor and each partner is different and should be treated as such. No one book or person can pretend to have all the answers. In many cases, you'll be forced to rely on your own ingenuity and good old-fashioned common sense to get through the tough times.

Having said all that, however, let's move on.

The Crisis Stage

As I mentioned at the beginning of this chapter, it's very important for the survivor to heal. In some way, the abuse always leaves its mark. Before we get into the crisis stage, however, I have to assume that the survivor has decided to heal. I have to assume that she's started on her journey by admitting that abuse did occur. The healing process is, in many ways, similar to that of an alcoholic. The survivor must admit the abuse occurred before she can move on. Once that hurdle has been cleared the other stages are sure to follow.

The crisis stage is a stage which can scare the living daylights out of you because it's usually the first time you see the survivor out of control. Until now, the survivor may have handled everything with relative calm. But in this stage, she doesn't know where to turn for help. Everything closes around her fast. She may cry a lot, be unable to do things on her own and want to give up. She may also start to question whether she's doing the right thing.

In our case, the crisis stage started not long after Liz had started her healing. She was facing the painful truth and it began to overwhelm her. Shock set in and she started to panic. I started to panic too. Liz began falling apart. She'd been doing so well until that point, but within a day she began drifting into a state of despair. She turned to me for help, a last-ditch effort to get out of her desperate state, but I didn't have any answers.

For the first time since she had started healing I really felt lost and helpless. I didn't know what to do. So, in desperation, I phoned the mental health ward at our local hospital and was put in touch with a counselor who explained to me what was happening. Just knowing it was normal to go through this stage was helpful in itself. I watched Liz closely for a few days, talked to her about her feelings, then got her to her counselor the following week. It worked. She made it safely through.

I learned you can be a big help in this stage by reassuring the survivor that she's doing the right thing and making sure she's safe. You can also help take some of the load off her by taking on some of her responsibilities, whether it be grocery shopping or taking care of the finances. If it's her job to take care of the garden or car, then maybe you can do that for her too. The point is to try and take the pressure off—some way, any way. She has enough to worry about while she's in a crisis, and relieving her of the other worries will help her tremendously.

There is one word of warning in all of this, however. Only take charge if the situation is desperate. It's important that the survivor retain control over her healing, even during the crisis stage. The survivor has to know that she got through the crisis on her own. You can help, but you also have to realize it's her fight in the end. The process of healing is also a process of re-empowerment for her.

What About Me?

The crisis stage is the time when most survivors think about suicide—something that is covered in greater detail in another chapter of this book. Don't fret too much about this stage, however. The important thing to remember is that the crisis stage doesn't last forever. And it shows the survivor is on the road to recovery. Once the survivor has accepted the reality of her situation, she'll deal with it and move on quickly to the next stage.

The Suffering Stage

The second or suffering stage is when the reality of everything that has happened sinks in. It is usually the longest stage. It can last for months, even years. It's the stage when the survivor comes to the realization that the abuse did happen and nothing can ever be the same again.

Common reactions during the suffering stage include nightmares, excessive fear, frequent memories of the abuse, and flashbacks, as if the abuse is happening all over again. During this stage, the survivor often has trouble with her memory, and has difficulty sleeping and concentrating on things. The survivor may feel isolated from other people and may lose her self-confidence. She may also have feelings of anger and rage—real rage. She'll also feel guilt, shame and depression.

Liz went through the whole range of feelings and emotions during this stage. One day she'd be fine, the next she'd be in a state of despair. It was like a never-ending cycle and I felt as if I was walking on eggshells half the time. Most of the time during this stage she didn't want to see anybody. She shunned her friends and didn't want to socialize. I'd try to boost her self-confidence because she didn't feel good about herself. She'd talk about moving to another city, just to escape having to deal with friends and workmates.

During this stage you may get tired of hearing about the abuse, but remember the victim needs to talk to someone in order to heal. This is a time when the survivor will go over and over the events of the abuse in her mind. One day things seem to be going fine and the next all hell breaks lose. At times during this stage, you'll feel like you're on a roller coaster that you can't get off. And in many ways you are. But, like everything else in the healing process, you'll just have to persevere and ride the roller coaster until it stops. You can't put a time limit on all this, but keep in mind it will end.

The suffering stage could be a very long one for the survivor—especially if she's having trouble working things out. And, though you need to give the survivor time to work things out, you can help by watching that she doesn't get stuck in a rut. If the survivor isn't working things out, or if the survivor is beginning to blame you for all her troubles, then professional help should be sought right away.

Time is the only sure way to tell if you're safely through this stage. It's only when you come across a prolonged period when the survivor is no longer trying to make sense out of all the childhood abuse that you can safely say you're at the end of the suffering stage.

The Resolution Stage

The resolution stage is perhaps the best of all three stages. That's because it's the final stage. But there are a few other reasons too. Everything just seems to start coming together here, to the great satisfaction of both you and the survivor. Finally, you get some rewards for all your hard work.

Although the survivor never forgets what happened to her, she does begin to put it in the right place—the past. The survivor may still talk about the abuse—and she always will—but the pain and anger she feels about it are gone. The survivor begins to treat the abuse as an experience, like any other in her life.

If she hasn't confronted the perpetrator by this time, she'll probably want to soon. She'll have determined by now what relationship, if any, she will have with her family. She'll have her life on track and she'll want to start learning all she can.

In many ways, it is a joy to watch the survivor as she reaches this stage. She is in control and deciding what she wants out of life. She'll begin making decisions about her future. She'll talk about her aspirations and goals. She'll be thinking of the times to come instead of the bad times in the past.

She may talk about making up for past losses, like school or work opportunities. She may contact old friends and try to re-establish relationships. She'll have a more positive outlook on life. She'll look towards challenges and might want to help others.

The survivor will be able to appreciate the everyday things in life. She'll be able to go to bed at night without having a fear of the dark. She'll be able to wake up in the morning without fear of the day ahead. She'll be able to go for a walk and truly enjoy the whole experience.

There will be no doubt in your mind when the survivor has reached this stage.

It will be unmistakable.

It will be remarkable.

She'll be the same person, yet different.

The difference will be wonderful.

Points to Remember

- Childhood sexual abuse always leaves its mark in some way.
- Healing is a necessary thing for the survivor.
- Healing from childhood sexual abuse takes time and courage.
- There are three main stages to healing—the crisis, suffering and resolution stages.

Chapter Three
It's Everywhere

Make no mistake. Child sexual abuse does exist. It's out there. It does happen—probably more often than you ever cared to imagine.

So believe it when your wife says she's been sexually abused. It may make you sick. It may turn your stomach. But it's all around us.

It's where you work, where you play, even where you spend your leisure time. You may already know many women who have been abused—at the office, at sports clubs and through friendships. They just haven't told you.

Our newspapers are filled with more and more stories about it. Every day we hear more about this heinous crime which has afflicted and invaded our society. The studies are now confirming what the experts have been telling us for decades—that it's a societal problem of major proportions, and it isn't getting any better.

More and more women are coming forward to confront the problem and the perpetrator. In the past, many women used to push the problem aside, saying, "It was only once that it happened," or "He was drunk." But now, they're coming forward in ever-increasing numbers.

Society used to try to sweep such crimes under the carpet. Rather than face the issue, many women used to keep it bottled up inside them. But now, as society's attitudes change from that of tolerance to abhorrence, more women are starting to report incidents to authorities. And the authorities are finally taking it seriously.

Reports of childhood sexual abuse have increased dramatically over the years and the experts agree we're only seeing the tip of the iceberg. A lot of people still don't come forward to report the problem. Often women aren't comfortable with disclosing that abuse occurred, because the family can have a very powerful influence on their lives and breaking the sanctity of the family is a taboo among many people.

Breaking the emotional ties with her family was one of the toughest things Liz has ever had to do in her life. Although abuse had occurred, her family was still close-knit. Telling me she was abused by a member of her family was a very unsettling experience for her. She was ostracized for stirring up trouble and taking her problems outside the family. But coming forward with the tale of abuse was her first real step towards freeing herself from the horrible past and unlocking all the anger which had kept her shackled.

Endless Numbers of Survivors

Ever so slowly and ever so painfully, more and more survivors like Liz are making their way from the shadows. They've started coming forward to tell their stories, to acknowledge the lost opportunities and the emotional damage that the years of abuse have caused.

It is difficult to gauge exactly how many women have been victims of childhood sexual abuse, molestation, gross indecency or incest. The statistics vary. But it's safe to say the number is in the millions. All the figures point to the fact that it's a problem of epidemic proportions.

One study, called the Badgley Report, found that one out of three girls and one out of six boys experience some form of unwanted sexual act by the time they reach the age of 18. The acts include witnessing an indecent exposure, being touched on a sexual part of the body, being sexually threatened or being subjected to an attempted or actual sexual assault.

The Badgley researchers also found:

- Two in one hundred young people had experienced attempted or actual acts of unwanted anal penetration by a penis or by means of an object or a finger.

- About one in four assailants was a family member or a person in a position of trust. About half were friends or acquaintances and about one in six was a stranger.
- Nearly all the assailants were males. One in one hundred was a female.
- Although the abuse was not typically characterized by violence, in the instances where violence occurred, it was very serious. More than two in five of all sexual assault homicides were committed against children 15 and younger.

The universally accepted figure is that one in every four women suffer from some form of sexual abuse at some point in their lives. That includes anything from touching, to incest, to a full-blown rape.

But findings from other studies indicate the rate of sexual violation could be much higher. Research findings from a study conducted throughout Canada indicated that one in two females and one in three males has been the victim of one or more unwanted sexual acts. About 80 per cent of those in the study were children when the offences occurred. A study conducted in San Francisco reported similar findings, concluding that half of all women are sexually assaulted before the age of 18.

The actual figures vary, but they all point to the fact it is a widespread problem. What you, as a supporter, have to remember is that young children are being sexually abused at an alarming rate. Sexual abuse happens to male and female children of every class, culture, religion and race. They're abused by parents, step-mothers and stepfathers, other relatives, family friends, babysitters, teachers and strangers. The other thing to remember is since not all victims report the crimes, they're being abused in much greater numbers than we think.

If we stick to the one in four figure, then, just imagine how many women, how many families, how many husbands and boyfriends are affected by all this. Imagine the toll in human suffering it has taken and will take, not only on the victims, but also on people like you—the supporters.

For the record, child sexual abuse can be any number of things. It can be:

- fondling or touching a child
- making sexual jokes or leering at a child
- masturbating or exposing in front of a child
- any type of sex with a child—oral, anal or intercourse
- stripping or sexually punishing a child
- taking naked pictures of a child or showing pornography to a child
- forcing children to have sex with each other

There is little doubt that child sexual abuse is a problem of major proportions in North America. It is evident by the lengthy waiting lists at counseling centres. Courts and child protection agencies are backlogged with cases of abuse. And the victims keep surfacing. Many don't even bother to come forward and report it to the authorities.

The whole issue isn't new, though. It's been around for years. Research shows that child sexual abuse first became an issue of concern in the late nineteenth century. Prostitution was flourishing in Paris and many of the women, most of whom were minors, began suffering from venereal disease, so politicians came up with laws aimed at putting a stop to the number of young girls being sexually abused.

Lately, with society's more liberal attitudes towards sex and talk about abuse, women's groups have begun pushing for acceptance of the fact that the crime exists and perpetrators should be punished severely. Their efforts have had some success and, as a result, the issue is finally receiving the attention that it truly deserves.

Rarely can you pick up a newspaper or turn on the television without hearing about it. Every day the media carry stories about children who have been abused. The media also provide us with court coverage of perpetrators being sentenced to jail time for their crimes. It's astounding some of the people who have been put under scrutiny lately—people we never imagined would do such things.

The Perpetrators

It seems that with better support systems now available, more and more survivors of childhood sexual abuse feel they can come forward, confront the perpetrator and then deal with the problems they've had.

Although child sexual abuse can involve physical force, it is estimated that two-thirds of the time it does not. A perpetrator usually uses emotional or psychological pressure to coerce the child into submission. The child's view of the perpetrator as an authority figure makes it much more likely that she can be threatened, bribed or manipulated into following orders.

The perpetrator may say things like "You're being a good girl if you do this," or "You know you'll get candy for doing such a good thing." Although children may sense what they are doing is wrong, they feel it is okay because they have assurances from the adult.

It may come as a shock that most child sexual abuse happens in so-called normal homes, but it's a fact supported by a number of studies. In fact, the image you may have of a typical perpetrator is probably wrong. In most cases, he's not a monster. If you stood in a crowd and tried to pick out the perpetrators you probably wouldn't have any luck. They are different, but their differences are hidden. For starters, at least 85 per cent of them are trusted relatives or acquaintances. Seldom are they dirty old men in soiled raincoats who sit on park benches. Seldom are they unshaven bums lurking near schoolyards, giving out candy to unsuspecting children. Seldom are they weirdos or sex-crazed strangers.

They're anybody and everybody. They could be your neighbors, friends, family members, co-workers or sports buddies. They're ministers, professionals, teachers. And, according to numerous stories we're hearing from the courts nowadays, the list does not stop there by any means.

At an orphanage in Newfoundland operated by the Christian Brothers, a Roman Catholic lay order, nine people were convicted of sex-related crimes after several orphans came forward with tales of abuse. In another case, a retired justice of the peace was charged with molesting two young people over a thirty-year period. He was 71 years old.

A committee which studied the problem in Canada found that one in four perpetrators were family members or a person in a position of trust. Half the assailants were friends of the victim and about one in six was a stranger. The statistics show that most molestations occur when the child is between the ages of 4 and 13 because that's when they are most vulnerable. They are still learning the rights and wrongs of life, don't know what sex is and still have blind trust in their elders.

Most victims are girls, although we're hearing more stories about boys also being victimized. Few are physically injured, but there is little doubt that the ordeal leaves them emotionally scarred for life.

What Else?

Well, studies have told us that the offenders are most often male. They may hold a white-collar job, blue-collar job or no job at all. Typically, they abuse their position of power in order to abuse the child. Most offenders aren't strangers to the child. Most are known to them as a relative—father, uncle, brother, grandfather, stepfather. They can also be a neighbor, family friend or even the babysitter. The perpetrator often commits the abuse in his own home or that of the child.

Studies have shown that child molestation doesn't just happen in impoverished families and in the geared-to-income housing subdivisions. It happens in the best of homes, and perpetrators are both rich and poor. It isn't limited to any social, economic or ethnic class. And there are no gender, cultural or religious boundaries.

About 95 per cent of the time the perpetrator gets that way because of the abuse or neglect he suffered as a child. They are usually troubled people with shredded self-esteem who need to dominate and have little understanding of the limits of normal behavior.

There is some good news in all of this, however. The statistics show that more and more perpetrators are being put behind bars. In fact, the number of inmates serving time in federal prisons for sexual offences against children has risen dramatically in recent years. Prison authorities maintain it's because more and more women are sticking up for their rights and coming forward with their stories.

Currently, about 21 per cent of the inmates in Canadian prisons for sex offences are behind bars because they committed acts against children. About 6 per cent of the sex offender inmates are in the prisons for incest convictions.

The statistics may be overwhelming at times. But one thing's for sure—the sexual assault of children will not go away because we ignore it. When your partner tells you she was victimized as a child—above all, believe her. She's not making it up, you can bet on that.

As a child, she probably didn't tell anybody because she was too afraid of what the perpetrator might do. It takes a lot of courage for a child to come forward and report something like sexual abuse.

Over the years, she may have wanted to tell somebody about the frightening things that were happening to her, but she may have had the feeling she wouldn't be believed or protected.

So now that she's told you don't confirm her worst fears and tell her to forget it. She can't and she won't. It's important that you believe her, show her you'll support her, protect her through thick and thin.

Instead of ignoring it, we have to acknowledge the existence of this very prevalent social disease. We have to use all of our resources to prevent it from happening again. It's a responsibility we must all share.

Points to Remember

- Childhood sexual abuse is a major problem.
- Millions of women have been victimized.
- More women are coming forward.
- Perpetrators come from all backgrounds.
- Don't ignore the problem.

Chapter Four
The Crisis Stage

The time will come. You can bet on it. It's very unfortunate, but no woman who is healing from the trauma of childhood sexual abuse can avoid it.

It's the crisis or emergency stage—a time in the healing process when everything in the survivor's life seems to fall apart at the seams.

It can be one of the most gut-wrenching and trying times for both you and the survivor. While she may experience feelings of helplessness and hopelessness, you may experience feelings of doubt and despair. It can be an especially frustrating time since you desperately want to help, but there isn't much you can do to take away her pain. You may get disheartened during this stage because you're an outsider looking in. It feels as if you have no control over the situation.

The crisis or emergency stage can come suddenly and without warning. Sometimes during the healing process too much happens too fast. There's just too much activity at once. The survivor is unable to handle it and gets overwhelmed by the whole process.

It's not difficult to figure out why this happens. During the initial stages of a survivor's healing, she focuses all her energy on bringing back the haunting memories of the abuse. It's something she must do, an unfortunate process that most survivors have to go through methodically and painfully in order to sort things out in their own minds.

When she's at this point in her healing, the survivor wants to remember everything that happened to her. She has to remember everything that happened in order to move on. But bringing all the memories back can also be a very traumatic experience for her, not to mention totally overwhelming. During this period of remembering, the survivor has to face up to the truth. And, if the perpetrator was somebody very close to the survivor, it can be an especially painful and trying experience for her.

It's a particularly difficult time for the survivor because she is trying to remember what she has tried to forget for so many years. It's something she tried to put into the back of her mind for a long time. Now, she desperately has to seek the missing pieces to the puzzle so that she can put them all together in her mind.

I remember how Liz used to talk for hours about her abuse. Once she got started, she wouldn't let it rest. In the early stages of her healing, the abuse seemed to haunt her everyday thoughts. She had to talk it out in order to make some kind of sense of it all. It was like mulling over a problem. She had to bounce her ideas and thoughts off of me, then put all the pieces to the puzzle back together again, this time in the right order.

She had tried for so many years to forget the abuse. She had tried for so many years to bury it so deep inside her that it would never surface again. Once she started remembering, however, it seemed it would never stop. It was a difficult time for us because, apart from the counselor she was seeing, Liz didn't have anybody else to share her stories with. I was her sole support and it made life particularly trying at times.

I found the best way to handle this was to take an interest in what she had to say. Rather than just wait for her to talk herself out, I really became interested in what she was telling me. I really got involved in conversations about her past and asked questions so I'd better understand it all. I think my taking an interest helped her make sense of it so much quicker. If she had to go through it by herself and make sense of it all by herself, I strongly believe it would have taken her much longer. Because I listened, I mean really listened, to what she was dealing with, I also learned more about what she was going through and that helped me too.

It's Overwhelming

The duration of the crisis stage depends on a number of things. For example, it depends on the severity and extent of the abuse, how old the survivor was when it happened and how clearly she can recall the acts of abuse. There are other factors too—like whether the perpetrator was in a position of trust and how often the abuse occurred.

The crisis stage can be overwhelming because the survivor is suddenly flooded with memories, but may not yet have the skills to cope with all the problems that also come with remembering the past. She may not yet have learned how to control her emotions, how to deal with them and still live a normal life. Sometimes all the emotional trauma which accompanies the flashbacks is just too much.

It's not surprising then, that you don't know how to react. All of a sudden the survivor is overwhelmed. It may be the first time you really see her out of control and you don't know how to help. It may also be the first time you find yourself without any real answers.

When the pressure really gets too much, the survivor might panic and even talk about suicide. She might also suggest not going any further with the healing or even ending her relationship with you.

I heard all three in the early days when Liz was healing. She'd get so upset with everything that she'd threaten to leave me. She'd vow never to see her counselor again. She'd say it's better to suffer in silence than go through the pain of healing from the abuse. She'd get so overwhelmed that she'd talk about running away from it all, starting a new life away from me and everybody else who knew about her situation.

A few times I was at my wit's end. I got tired of hearing her continually threaten to leave. It just wasn't fair to me. When she started talking like that I used to leave her alone to gather her thoughts. I didn't argue with her. I didn't run away from it either. I just gave her the time and space she needed to sort things out. It always worked out in the end. She knew she really didn't want to leave because I wasn't the problem. The problem was inside herself and she just needed the time alone to come to grips with that. Once she was ready to talk again, we'd sit and discuss the problems she had.

The key here, as is so often the case with the healing process, is to try to remember it's all part and parcel of her getting better. Like all the other steps in the healing process, look upon the crisis or emergency stage as a step forward. It's something that is necessary for the survivor to go through. Any time someone heals from a traumatic experience, they go through a stage where they get overwhelmed by all the problems.

Liz would go through a whole range of emotions. At times, she'd go through a stage where she didn't believe it had happened to her. Other times, she'd want to do everything she could to heal faster. There was no way you could tell on any given day how she'd feel.

It's Normal

It is important to remember that it's quite natural for a person who is healing from childhood sexual abuse to go through this type of emotional upheaval. It's not out of the ordinary for a survivor to have very different thoughts and feelings on different days.

During the crisis stage, the survivor might be unable to cope with her feelings or she might act in a very disoriented manner. She might have very strong emotions or none at all. She might suffer physical symptoms like loss of appetite. But, once again, it is a progression for her. The survivor has to go through the crisis stage in order to deal with her past, sort it out and go on with her future. You might want to remind yourself of that when things get tough.

And, for heaven's sake, try not to panic during the emergency stage. Two panicky people won't do any good. You've got a very important job to do here. It's not much use having two people unable to cope, running around like chickens with their heads cut off. Remember, you're supposed to help her. You can be a steadying influence. You can see that she gets through this stage safely and without causing any harm to herself.

It can be really tough, there's no doubt about that. Although the survivor may be a strong person, it's likely that her defenses will be very low at this point. The crisis or emergency stage will be the time she really needs your help the most. It's so important to her. Don't be surprised to find the survivor leaning on you a lot during this stage. This is also the time when the survivor may be in dire need of help from a professional. It's best to try and talk about this before it happens. It's best if the survivor has agreed to let you seek help for her if she gets to a point where she can't cope. But it doesn't always work out that way. Often survivors and supporters haven't laid out the ground rules. If you get to this point and find the survivor is in real trouble, ask the survivor if she wants help. If she does, don't wait. Seek that help for her right away.

I was lucky during this stage. Liz had already been seeing a counselor and when times got tough all she had to do was book another appointment. She'd average one session a week during the initial stages of her healing. Eventually, it tapered off to once a month as she progressed in her healing until one day we went to the counselor and had nothing to talk about. We knew then it was time to go it alone.

We visited the counselor together. She had a few sessions on her own, but for the most part we agreed it would be better if I knew exactly what was going on. I also found that I better understood how to deal with the situation if I had more knowledge of the process.

You should never be worried or embarrassed at being unable to handle the healing process by yourself. Don't hesitate to go to a counselor, mental health clinic or a nearby hospital if you need the help. That's what they're there for. Once you go, you'll probably find they're not such bad places after all. The staff in clinics and hospitals are very caring. The medical profession has come a long way in helping people who have emotional difficulties.

My experience is that staff are well qualified and very willing to help survivors who may find themselves in a crisis. They've not only been trained clinically but they likely also have years of on-the-job training in how to deal with such matters. Their advice and help can prove invaluable.

Don't worry about what people think. For one thing, nobody will know if you don't tell them. If you do tell somebody you or the survivor have been to a mental health clinic or counselor, though, make sure it is a friend—a true friend. You don't want everybody in the neighborhood discussing your business over a cup of tea.

Liz and I rarely told anybody we were seeing a counselor. I was a reporter at the local newspaper and didn't want our problems to be known. Liz didn't want people feeling sorry for her. It's strange how people's opinions of you change once they find out you're seeking help. There's another very good reason, though. It seems when people find out you're seeing a counselor, that's all they want to talk about. Others often start to lay their problems on you. They feel they can share their similar experiences with you, something that doesn't help when you are trying to deal with the after-effects of abuse.

You know the survivor better than anybody, so there's little doubt that you're in the best position to offer assistance if she's having trouble deciding whether or not she needs professional help. The survivor might have a tough time deciding on her own. Either she is hesitant to trust anyone she doesn't know or she thinks she's weak or a failure if she gives in to professional help. That's nonsense, however, and you know it. Nobody should be expected to get through the healing process on their own. If the survivor appears to be needing professional help, discuss it with her. Don't hesitate to talk to her about it if you think she's ready to reach out.

Finding a good counselor is one of the most important jobs that you, as a supporter, can help with. Word of mouth is the best way of finding someone who can do the job, someone whom you can trust to help the survivor heal. If you know someone who has been through the process, don't be afraid to ask them for the name of a counselor. They'll likely be more than helpful in pointing you in the right direction. Failing that, try the yellow pages. Look under marriage and family therapists. That's where most of them are listed. Call the local police department, family counseling center or sexual assault center—they'll also have names of counselors available. Don't do anything without the survivor's permission, however. It wouldn't be any use for the survivor to go somewhere she doesn't want to be or see someone she doesn't particularly like. Make sure that you do everything in consultation with the survivor.

A counselor is like a good friend. The survivor has to trust the counselor. Remember, that doesn't happen in one visit. It takes time for the counselor to earn the survivor's trust. Give the counselor a chance to earn that friendship. If, after several visits, the survivor still doesn't like the counselor, the two of you should not be afraid to change to another. If the survivor does want to change counselors, however, make sure she's doing it for all the right reasons.

Here are some of the right reasons for changing counsellors:
- The survivor can't seem to open up to the counselor.
- The counselor doesn't seem interested in what the survivor has to say.
- The counselor seems to be going too fast for the survivor.
- The counselor is abusive to the survivor.
- The counselor has so many clients the survivor can't book regular appointments.
- The survivor gets a bad feeling about the counselor.

Suffice it to say, it's always better to err on the side of caution if you think the survivor needs professional help—in other words, strongly suggest getting help. If she refuses, try talking to her about the situation. Keep a close eye on her all this time and, if she does get to the point again where you can suggest the option, try again and see what the response is. Keep trying, but don't keep nagging her every five minutes. That won't do either of you any good. She'll get too used to refusing and eventually she won't even think about what you're asking.

In most cases, though, if a survivor is at a real loss as to where to turn for help, she will go to see a professional if you suggest that option to her, not too forcefully. Remember, she doesn't need anybody pushing her around at this stage. Suggest, but don't order her. Somebody who is in real emotional pain will jump at any opportunity to rid themselves of the anguish and suffering they're feeling if the option is presented to them in the right manner and not forced down their throat. It's certainly better if she goes of her own free will. She'll get more out of the advice from the professionals.

It Will End

There is no set time for a survivor to remain in the emergency or crisis stage. As with the rest of the healing, the survivor may work through a crisis, and go on to another stage of her healing, only to find herself one day thrust back unmercifully into the crisis stage. Sure, it's disappointing to you and her, but each time she takes a step back she'll likely end up taking two steps forward in the long run. Be ready for this to happen because it does often, especially near the beginning of the healing process.

Liz would go through a period where everything would be rosy. Her recovery seemed imminent. But the bubble would always burst. Something would happen that would trigger a relapse. She'd be doing so well, then just as quickly slip back into a world filled with problems. It was frustrating to watch, equally frustrating to experience, but it was all part of the process, as she'd eventually get on the right track again and move forward.

The crisis stage can be worse for some survivors than others. Some can get through it merely with the support of someone like yourself. Others require lengthy periods of professional help. How much professional help a survivor needs and for how long depends on many things. It depends on the emotional state of the survivor, how clearly she remembers the abuse, the type of job she might have, how much time she can devote to healing, whether she has a family and has to devote a lot of her time to others, what type of supports she has and how much natural ability she has to cope with hard times.

When a survivor begins to remember all the abuse that occurred in the past, it consumes her thoughts, all her waking hours—and sometimes her sleeping hours as well. It can flood a survivor's memory. She may never get to rest without thinking about it. Her thoughts and feelings may suddenly overwhelm her to the point where she can't cope.

The best thing you, as a supporter, can do during this stage is to try to keep things as stable as possible. Give her a solid base to work from. Sounds simple, but it's no easy task by any means, especially when your whole world looks as if it's going to fall apart at the seams.

It isn't easy to keep cool when the survivor is talking about taking her own life. It isn't easy to keep cool when you aren't prepared. It isn't easy to keep cool when you can't find answers and you can't see any improvements in the way things are going.

It's a very tough stage for all these reasons. In fact, it's likely the toughest stage in the whole healing process because it comes upon the two of you so quickly, so suddenly. You're eased gradually into the other stages. When the survivor was having flashbacks, you knew she was having flashbacks and were ready to comfort her. You got a chance to feel comfortable. But it just doesn't happen that way with the crisis stage. The crisis stage hits you without warning.

You really have to be on your toes here because you'll have to deal with a lot fast. Although the healing process looks like it has taken a turn for the worse at this stage, try and think of it as a step forward. The survivor has to go through this stage in order to heal. The sooner, the better—for both of you.

Getting Through It

Perhaps the best weapons you have to deal with this stage are foresight and knowledge. Sometimes just knowing the stage will come and go makes it easier on both of you. Knowing you will make it through this stage is also a big help. Talking with the survivor and lending her your supportive ear are the best things you can do during the crisis stage. Often the survivor just needs someone to talk to, someone who will sit and listen to her story. It may sound rather simple, but it is perhaps the best medicine for what's on her mind.

It's so important that the survivor get the bad out of her before she can replace it with good. During the crisis stage, that's exactly what's happening. She's remembering the bad. And, with proper help and counseling, the survivor will be able to have the effects of those bad memories drawn out of her in a safe manner. Eventually, that void will be replaced with positive, good experiences, normal experiences.

I remember the counselor telling Liz and me that she'd eventually replace all the bad experiences with good ones. When Liz first started healing all she had was anger and bitterness inside her. Now that she's healed, however, she can truly enjoy life. She has the ability to give love to others now that she knows what it truly is.

As a supporter, you probably won't be too happy going through the crisis stage, but try to keep in mind—again—that it's a very positive step. It's a traumatic but very important stage in the healing process, and the survivor has a better chance of getting through it if you are totally committed to going the distance with her and giving her the proper support, encouragement and help that she needs.

You can't be angry here. You can't be sad or impatient. The survivor won't be able to hurry herself through this period just for your sake. So relax and take a deep breath. You'll need some patience, real patience, understanding and a lot of compassion. Talk to the survivor. Remember, she's going through a tough time in her healing and you know by now that it doesn't come to pass overnight.

There is one word of warning here, though. Don't get sucked into her anger. Don't get angry with her. It's good to talk with her about her anger, but it doesn't do any good to be angry with her. It doesn't do any good to have two angry people trying to deal with their feelings. Also, be very careful not to become the object of her anger. Remember, she's looking for a place to vent her frustrations during this stage. She's looking for a place to blow off some steam and you'll likely be the prime target for her if you don't watch yourself.

A lot of survivors lose control during the crisis stage. They lash out at whoever they can. They also make a lot of mistakes, alienating loved ones or friends just because they had an anger session. If this is happening, all the more reason to direct her to professional help.

Remember not to push her too hard. She'll only resent that. Don't hold her back either. Instead try to calm her with rational talk—when the time is right, that is. Last of all, try to let her know that you're there for her, even if she is really angry.

No, it's not an easy task by any means. Then again, nobody said it was. So don't panic. She'll pull through this stage. And so will you.

Points to Remember

- The crisis stage comes on suddenly.
- It's a traumatic but very important stage in the recovery process.
- Suggest counseling if you feel your partner needs it.
- Don't panic—the crisis stage will pass.

Chapter Five
The Hidden Taboo

Suddenly, pangs of fear grip your body. The survivor is talking about suicide—the hidden taboo—and you have no idea how to react. You haven't talked about it before. You haven't thought about it before. The survivor might have had depressions, but suicide never crossed her mind. It's no wonder, then, that you're a little taken aback when the word is mentioned.

Just the mere mention of suicide is enough to strike fear into the heart of any supporter. After all, you've probably worked long and hard with the survivor for some time now, been through hell and back, only to see her start making threats about taking her own life. It's little wonder that you're upset. You might even have thought the survivor was making some headway in her healing, when, all of a sudden, here she is talking about ending her life.

Liz mentioned suicide many times during her healing process, and each time she did, my stomach would go into knots. She worked so hard on her healing, and then suddenly she would say she just wanted to end it all. I recall feeling angry when she mentioned taking her own life. But later, Liz would tell me she had really just been crying out for help. She didn't really want to take her own life. She was just so overwhelmed about everything going on around her. It was her way of saying she needed to try to get rid of the pain she was feeling.

The lesson here is not to take it personally. Don't get angry with the survivor for thinking about suicide. It won't do any good. Keep your job in perspective here. Remember, your priority is to support the survivor through the ordeal and worry about your feelings later on. There will be time enough afterwards to talk and work out your feelings on this issue when the danger of her taking her own life has passed.

What About Me?

Reaching Out for Help

When a survivor tells you she is thinking about suicide, keep in mind that what she's really doing is reaching out for help. She's probably reached the stage in her healing process when she's given up everything and it doesn't look like there will ever be an end to it all. When Liz was suicidal, she'd have such a dismal outlook on life, there was very little I could do to cheer her up. She'd tell me that nothing mattered. She'd say there was nothing good in the world. She'd say life wasn't worth living. She'd say how nice it would be to die and go to a place where there were no problems. She didn't really care what I, or anybody else, thought about her at that point.

It was very traumatic to see her like this, but I'd keep the conversation rolling and eventually we'd get into discussions about the people and things that were important to us in life. The longer we talked, the more she'd begin to appreciate life again.

Supporters should do their best not to get too frazzled when the subject of suicide is mentioned. Suicide is an act to avoid the pain of living as much as it is a desire to die. It's common for survivors to have thoughts of suicide when they're trying to deal with the traumatic loss of their childhood. It's like grieving for someone who has passed away. Often people who have lost someone get depressed after the reality of the loss sinks in. It's the same way with the survivor. Once she starts dealing with the loss of her childhood, she can become sad and depressed. It's quite normal behavior for a survivor.

Like someone who is grieving, the survivor needs time to feel and deal with the pain of her own loss. Remember, she has lost her childhood. She needs time to grieve that loss. So when she tells you she doesn't want to live, she's not crazy or mentally retarded. She doesn't need someone telling her she shouldn't feel that way. What she needs is someone who will sit and listen to her and not judge her.

It would be more dangerous for her to deny that the suicidal thoughts ever existed. If she pushed them away and didn't deal with them, talk about them to somebody, they would continue to haunt her.

Always Take It Seriously

Survivors who express suicidal thoughts should always be taken seriously. Don't brush your partner off if she tells you she's thinking about taking her own life. Telling you she has suicidal thoughts doesn't necessarily mean she really wants to take her own life. Perhaps she merely wants someone to take away the awful pain that she is feeling.

Talk of suicide is often an extension or consequence of feeling miserable, lonely, depressed and in despair. Believe, however, that the survivor is having trouble dealing with some type of loss. Never ignore the conversation and think the thoughts will pass on their own. Don't, for example, say, "Okay, honey. Just get some sleep and we'll talk about it in the morning when you're feeling a little better." You can bet she won't be feeling any better in the morning, and you can bet you'll be the last person she ever comes to if she needs help again.

When the window of opportunity is there, you have to keep it open. When the survivor tells you she's thinking about suicide, she really needs someone to talk to, so you have to take some steps to help.

I clearly remember one night sitting in bed with Liz when she broke down in tears and told me how she had thought about suicide that day. She said she had been fighting an inner battle for weeks and didn't want to tell me about it because she didn't want to mess up my life. It was clear she was in dire straits, so I got out a pen and paper and asked her to list the reasons she should live and the reasons she should not, and I would do the same. At first she was reluctant to make out a list, but eventually she agreed. It wasn't the list that was important—although I made sure I thought of more reasons she should live—it was the fact that we began discussing the things in life that were important to her and the reasons she should live. Even now, that night is clearly etched in her memory.

What About Me?

When a survivor tells you she is suicidal, think of yourself as a lifeguard. She's really trying to tell you that she's drowning and needs some help to stay afloat.

You Know Her Best

Deciding how serious a survivor is about committing suicide is a tough thing to do. But you're in the best position to find out. You know her better than anybody. You know what she's like when she's normal and you can probably be a good judge of how disturbed and serious she is about the whole thing when she's upset.

People who are seriously thinking about committing suicide usually communicate their plans, either directly or indirectly, through hints and clues.

Some of the warning signs include:
• talking about suicide
• a deep or prolonged depression
• feelings of helplessness or hopelessness
• extreme mood changes or odd behavior
• saying things like "You'll be better off without me" or "All of my problems will soon be gone"
• giving away prized possessions and getting affairs in order
• loss of interest in work or hobbies
• isolation from friends and colleagues
• loss of appetite or sexual desire
• disturbed sleep periods
• lack of interest in appearance

If you think the survivor is suicidal but she hasn't come out and told you, the best thing to do is simply ask her. If you're picking up signals from her, it's the best way to clear the air.

Don't be afraid of putting thoughts in her head. Asking the survivor to tell you the truth won't make her decide to commit suicide. And once the truth is out, don't be surprised by what you hear. Healing from childhood sexual abuse is a traumatic experience and in many cases it's accompanied by overwhelming feelings of loss, anxiety and frustration—the perfect mix to cause someone to think about suicide.

In most cases, the survivor who is thinking about suicide just wants to be dead for the time being. So when you're first confronted with it—don't panic. This is a chance to really help the survivor. Don't be afraid of what she's telling you. If you feel her suicidal intentions are strong, seek consent to get her professional help right away. If you have any reason to believe the survivor might actually commit suicide, keep a close eye on her so that she's unable to carry it out. One way to judge the seriousness of the situation is to ask her if she has a plan. If she does, then she's likely serious. In such desperate situations, do your best to convince her to seek professional help right away. Always respect her wishes and feelings. If she resists professional help, listen to her and try to figure out what is triggering her suicidal thoughts. Ask her why she won't see a professional. It could very well be that she has a fear or distrust of counselors. She might have had a bad experience in the past. Whatever the reason, don't question what she's thinking; just listen. Empathize with her pain. Don't take sides either; that won't help. Just listen and keep her talking about her thoughts. As long as you're listening she's not going to take her own life.

There are a number of other ways to determine how serious a survivor is about taking her own life. For example, consider if anyone in the survivor's family has committed suicide or whether the survivor has made previous suicide attempts. Even a mild suicide attempt, such as swallowing a bottle of sleeping tablets, indicates a desperate need for understanding.

Psychiatrists use a number of criteria to determine whether a person is at risk of committing suicide. Their list assesses such things as whether the person has dreams of catastrophes, whether they are unemployed and whether they are depressed or have a tendency to complain continuously.

Of course, it goes without saying that it is wise to err on the side of caution if you think a survivor may be serious about taking her own life. One thing you should do, whether you believe her or not, is enter into a pact with her. Ask the survivor to agree she won't harm herself until she's got some professional help. By making a deal with her, you've alleviated the immediate threat until someone with more experience in these matters can deal with the survivor.

How to Help

If the survivor has confirmed she is considering suicide then get in touch with the police or a suicide hotline or call your local hospital. Remember, you won't get in trouble for trying to help. You're trying to save the survivor's life.

If you begin to feel yourself getting angry at the survivor, try to remember she's not doing this intentionally to harm or hurt you in any way. All she's trying to do is find a way to rid herself of some of the pain she's feeling. The survivor is dealing with a tremendous loss at this stage. She could be dealing with the loss of childhood, the loss of a family, the loss of her innocence—all significant and painful experiences.

Whatever the case, you can bet she's feeling a significant loss, something that tugs on her emotions and is leaving her with a sense of helplessness, hopelessness and frustration. To help the survivor, try to listen to what she's really saying. Don't just nod your head, but really listen and get involved in the conversation. If the survivor feels you really do care and are willing to help her work through her feelings, share some of her pain, then she won't feel so much alone and will realize she truly has someone on her side.

It's important to try to communicate at this stage, but don't give any advice. Let the survivor figure things out for herself. You can talk with her, open her mind to possibilities, but don't make the decision for her. She has to come to the conclusion on her own. It's the only way she'll truly get the feelings out of her system.

When you talk to a survivor who is considering suicide, try to help her realize that life is worth living. Talk about the things that are important to her, the things that interest her. Ask her what she'd like to do or talk about. Perhaps she'll want to set some goals for herself. Perhaps she'll just want to vent all her frustrations.

You'll have to use your intuition here. There is no strict set of guidelines to follow which will make a survivor start feeling better. As a supporter, though, you're in the best position to notice the signs of distress and help the survivor get over her crisis. You know her better than anybody. You know what makes her feel good about herself. You're the person she trusts. Rest assured that with your help, she'll make it through.

Points to Remember

- Don't get upset when suicide is mentioned.
- Always take it seriously.
- Watch for the warning signs.
- Always err on the side of caution.
- Empathize with her.
- Seek professional help if she wants it.
- Don't be angry with her.

Chapter Six
To Stay or Go

It's been a bad day. The survivor is crying. You're feeling pretty bad about yourself. The two of you have just had a real big blowout. You've said some nasty things. So did she. Now, you're angry, frustrated and left wondering what to do. She's in the same boat.

Just last week, the same thing happened. You sat there with the same questions going through your mind. How did you get into such a mess? How are you going to see it all through? Should you try to make up? Or should you just get your things and leave?

Yes, it's a toughie. You may have tried to work things out, only to see the relationship crumble before your eyes. At this point it may seem as if there's nothing you can do. The unfortunate part is that it's a situation many supporters find themselves in and, unfortunately, it's also a situation for which there are no easy answers.

This is the one where you're sort of on your own. You and you alone can come up with the final answer. Only you can dig deep, really deep, reflect inside yourself, and then determine whether helping the survivor heal is what you really want to do. Sure, it's a noble cause, a noble thing to think about doing. But by now you probably realize it takes a lot of time, commitment and energy, lots of energy.

Whether you stay or leave the relationship is strictly your own decision. Nobody else can decide this one for you, nor should they try. It's a very personal decision. You'll have to dig deeper than you've ever dug before.

You should realize that helping someone recover from the effects of childhood sexual abuse is taxing. It's a process that will draw heavily on all your strengths, it's a process that will exploit all your weaknesses and it's a process that will test all of your resources. It's time-consuming, it's exhausting, and the rewards are few and far between. Just when you think you've got it licked, the problem will rear its ugly head again. It wears you down. It can be frustrating. It can make life miserable.

It's a process that is painful, frightening and infuriating, to say the least. The survivor's moods can swing unpredictably. You never know what to expect. One minute things are fine, the next all hell starts to break loose. The emotions you experience go from happiness to sadness, from hope to helplessness.

It shouldn't come as a surprise, then, that most supporters think about leaving a relationship many times during the healing process. It also shouldn't come as a surprise that many relationships in which a spouse has chosen to deal with the sexual abuse of her past end up on the rocks. The pressure it brings is tremendous.

I remember Liz telling me about the survivors in her support group. One of their biggest complaints was the men in their lives. Most of the women felt their supporters weren't doing enough to help them. They were more of a bother than a help. The men weren't listening to them, they weren't able to cope with the problems the survivors were going through. They were demanding too much of the survivors.

Most of the women in the group felt their relationships were on the rocks. They didn't expect their relationships to last much longer. The men, it seems, just didn't understand their predicaments. The survivors said the men were giving them so many problems they really didn't care whether they stayed or left.

Don't Feel Guilty

It's no secret that every relationship has its problems at times. Even under normal circumstances it's difficult to get two people to agree on things all the time. So, under more difficult circumstances, you can see why it can be even more trying. With the divorce rate looming around 50 per cent, it doesn't take a genius to figure out that not all marriages are working out—even under normal circumstances.

Don't feel guilty, then, when you're thinking about leaving a relationship with a survivor. It's a completely normal thing to consider. After all, so many things change when you have to deal with someone who is healing from childhood sexual abuse. Your life is radically different than before.

It might be wise to take a good, hard, close look at this question early in the healing process, before you get in too deep. It's a question you'll probably also want to think about many times as you go through the process. Don't think you're losing your marbles. You're quite sane. Whatever you decide, you will feel better about it in the long run.

Now, that may sound a little confusing to you so let me explain. If you've given yourself the time to think about the situation and you decide to stay, then you're doing so with a clear conscience. You're ready, with that same clear conscience—having freely decided to stay—to tackle any of the problems associated with the healing. If, by the same token, you decide to leave, it will also be with a clear conscience, because you've thoroughly examined all the options.

Either decision then—no matter how difficult and painful it may seem—will be for the betterment of both parties. There's no use staying with something that shows signs of never working out for you, is there?

While only you can weigh the options and decide, there are a few things to think about as you're pondering this. There are good reasons and bad reasons to leave a relationship with a survivor, just as there are good reasons and bad reasons to stay with a survivor.

Here are some good reasons to leave:
- The survivor has become abusive herself or has turned to dependency on alcohol or drugs to get her through the trauma of the ordeal.
- You have grown so far apart and have such different interests that you know in your heart that even when the survivor heals from the abuse of her childhood, you won't have any desire to stay.
- You no longer trust each other.
- You've found someone else in your life.

Here are some bad reasons to leave:

- Your partner is spending so much time in therapy and taking care of her own problems that she doesn't have the time for you and your problems.
- Your partner is changing and just isn't the same person she used to be.
- You need some more excitement in your life and you're tired of talking about abuse all the time.

It's a good idea to think about some of these questions as you make your final decision. Don't try to stay in a relationship in which the survivor tries to harm you or herself. It won't do either of you any good to stay together under those circumstances. It will only lead to bitterness, hostility and more violence between the two of you. It's best to walk away if something like that happens. Your own welfare is important here too.

Whatever you do, though, take your time to make the decision. Don't rush into anything. Remember that emotions are running rampant and there are a lot of outside pressures you're dealing with.

I remember countless times sitting on the front porch, feeling absolutely lousy about myself and my predicament. It wasn't any one thing that caused me to feel like this. All the small problems associated with the healing process just built up every so often and it was important for me to sit and reflect on what I really wanted out of life. Sometimes I'd sit there for hours just thinking about what was important. I'd make lists, write down the good and bad reasons to stay and good and bad reasons to leave. It must have been in the cards to stay, because at the end of each thinking session I'd have made up my mind that I wanted to stay with Liz and support her during the healing process. It was sort of like recharging the batteries and clearing your head for the work still to be done.

Why Me?

When you're thinking about all this, you have to be cautious about what I call the "why me" syndrome. It can creep into the relationship as you go through the healing process with a survivor.

What About Me?

You know it's there when you start wondering why all this is happening to you, why you've been put into this situation. Your friends and family can add to that pressure. They may start to reinforce the "why me" syndrome by asking, "Why is this happening to you? Why are you in this situation?"

All this can weigh on your conscience, and coping with all the pressure can be devastating. You can't avoid feeling sorry for yourself at times. But you can be aware of it so when it happens you know it's there and you're ready to deal with it effectively and move on.

This book can't list a specific set of rules which will determine whether you should stay or leave a relationship. Nobody can do that. No rules can be set in stone as to what determines whether you should stay or leave. Each person is different. That's what makes life so interesting. Each person has their own limits. You'll have to decide yours.

But there are some general guidelines you can follow in deciding whether to stay or leave. First, you're going to have to be very honest with yourself during this phase. You're going to have to take some time out for yourself, dig deep and truly decide if you want to go through the process of helping a survivor heal herself. Decide if it's really worth your while to stay in a relationship with a survivor who is healing. Think about what's at the end of it for you.

Now, that may sound selfish, but it's not. Everybody has to think a bit about their well-being. After all, there's no use staying with someone who might not care for you after the healing is finished, is there?

Should you weather the punches or throw in the towel? It's a tough question. It's not easy to decide. You have to determine whether you have the patience, love and sheer willpower to go through the healing with the survivor. You've got to make some hard choices. You've got to be honest. But you have to decide.

When I found these thoughts entering my head, I'd tell Liz I was going out for a few hours to think. Usually, I would just get in the car and drive to a spot near the river where I would sit with my coffee and do some serious reflecting. With nobody around to distract me, I was in a totally relaxed environment where I could think of my options. It's good to get away sometimes and do this because it helps you keep everything in perspective. Often you can get so wrapped up in the healing process, you can't take an objective look at yourself and the way things are going. Getting away for some quiet time by myself—even if it was only for a couple of hours—helped me find answers to the questions.

Food for Thought

There are a number of things you should consider when you're pondering all this. You should think about whether you can take rejection—from your wife and, at times, from your family, friends and co-workers. Are you strong enough, and willing, to keep going on your own?

There's still a stigma attached to childhood sexual abuse, don't think there isn't. Many people feel it shouldn't be spoken about, that it should be kept within the family. The issue shakes the very roots of morality and many people don't want to face it. It's an unfortunate part of life, but a lot of people simply don't believe it's such a common occurrence. You're going to have to deal with these issues and it's important you think about them now, rather than later.

Deciding if you have the time and patience to handle it all is one of the tough decisions you're going to have to make. You may have other commitments that prevent you from putting all your efforts and energies into helping your wife or partner heal. You may not be the type of person who can deal with any more pressures. You may simply not want to go through it. Whatever the case, be honest with yourself.

Also, don't do it in a day and don't make this decision when you're angry. If you're thinking about leaving, be honest with the survivor. When things cool down, tell her you have to do some thinking about the relationship. Don't leave her in the dark. She has enough to think about without trying to guess what's happening with you.

What About Me?

Be honest with her about your feelings. As soon as you know what you want to do, tell her. If you're thinking about leaving, schedule some time to think about this, make the decision and then act on it. Perhaps you need a weekend at the cottage by yourself. Perhaps a day at the beach would help. Perhaps just working around the garden might give you the time you need to think it through and sort things out.

But, if you decide to stay, then stay. Don't threaten her. Don't say things like "I'll stay if you straighten up your act" or "If you don't get things together, I'm leaving." She probably won't respond to threats, nor should she. Remember that what she's feeling inside controls her and nothing you say or do is going to speed up that process.

If, after careful thought, you decide you must leave, then tell the survivor directly. After all, you owe that much to her. You wouldn't like to be left in the dark over such an important matter; neither does she. Remember, she's not going through the healing process to bug you. She's doing it because it's something she just has to do. It drives her.

If you're leaving, don't give her a false impression about why you're leaving. She won't buy it. Make sure you're honest and forthright with her. Don't stay in the relationship just because she's dealing with the abuse. That's a bad move. A bad relationship won't help her in the long run. Take solace in the fact you've probably helped her in some small way already.

If you leave, there's no doubt that she'll miss you and mourn the loss. But rest assured that the survivor won't fall apart. She will survive. She may have some tough times dealing with the loss of you, but once she has started on the road to recovery, it's very difficult for her to stop. She may take a few wrong turns at times, but for the most part she'll press forward—with or without your help.

If you are leaving, then leave. And do it with a clean conscience, knowing that you've done your best. You've probably even gained from the experience. You know now what the world of the child abuse survivor is like.

But if you stay—then stay. And commit yourself fully to

going through the healing process with the survivor. It may take time, but you'll likely be glad you did.

Points to Remember

- It's normal to think about leaving.
- The decision is yours and yours alone.
- Be absolutely honest with yourself.
- Take the time to make a proper decision.
- If you decide to stay, then stay. If you decide to go, then go.
- Don't feel guilty about your decision.

Chapter Seven
The Child Within

It's a strange concept. Bizarre, to say the least. You'll be sitting there, talking to the survivor, when all of a sudden you realize she isn't even listening. Instead, she'll be staring at some faraway object as though deep in thought.

At that moment, you wonder if she's losing her marbles. She's not. And neither are you. The survivor is merely getting in touch with a part of herself that hasn't healed. It's something deep inside her called the child within—something that's been with her for years.

She's never seen it, probably never talked to it and likely didn't know it existed. But it's probably always been there—locked somewhere in the crevices of her mind. And now that she's started the healing process, it's come to the forefront. It wants attention and it wants it now.

The child within is one of the most difficult things for supporters to understand, but it's also something you'll probably have to come to grips with.

For the survivor, the child is a real thing, although not in the physical sense. The survivor is able to feel what the child feels, talk to it, even console it. Sometimes the survivor can picture the child inside her. She can see her sitting in a room, playing with her things.

Usually the child resembles what the survivor thinks she looked like as a child. At times, the survivor will be totally in touch with the child within. Other times, she'll be completely at its mercy.

I've been told by some therapists that survivors sometimes don't have a child within. In other cases, the child just doesn't come out. It depends a lot on the severity and nature of the abuse. Usually, a survivor can only be put in touch with the feelings of the child through therapy.

One time Liz was having such trouble dealing with the child within that she got angry and literally yelled at it. She just wanted the child to go away and never bother her again. The child did disappear but only for a while. I remember how worried we were at what had happened. Liz and I both knew that the child within would return. We just weren't sure what damage we had caused. We were worried about what would happen when it did return. Sure enough, the child did come back with a vengeance. Like a spoiled child, it demanded more attention than ever.

Accepting the Child

There are many supporters who have trouble accepting this strange phenomenon. It's no small wonder. If you ever told anybody about it, they'd think you're crazy to say the least. They'd probably think the survivor is crazy too.

For them, it may conjure up images of Sybil, the girl with the umpteen different personalities. It doesn't exactly work that way, but try and tell that to those who don't know much else about childhood sexual abuse. They won't understand.

I remember countless times when Liz would be dealing with the child within. At first, I just shied away from the whole thing and trusted her to deal with the situation. But eventually, she began to trust me enough that she'd let me in on what was going on. If Liz was in the process of dealing with the child within, she'd talk to me about it and ask for my opinion. I was always careful not to insult the child. After all, this was an entity that had been abused and there was no point in ridiculing the child for something that wasn't her fault. The child eventually grew such trust for me that I could talk to it. Sounds a bit nuts, doesn't it? I'd talk to Liz, who would relay the message to the child and give me an answer. I wouldn't recommend this for every supporter, but if you feel comfortable enough doing this, I don't think there's any real harm in it.

If you think about it for a moment, it's not all that complicated or startling that the child who is abused doesn't develop normally. Think about how old the survivor was when she was abused. Now picture yourself about that age. Ask yourself how you would have felt if someone you trusted had come into your room in the middle of the night and abused you. Remember, you didn't know anything about sex. You didn't know if it was right or wrong. How would it have affected your emotional development? How would it have affected your trust for people? How would it have affected your self-confidence and your own self-worth?

The extent of psychological damage can vary widely, depending on the abuse. It depends, for example, on how long the abuse continued and on the relationship of the offender to the child. It also depends on such things as the kind and degree of sexual abuse, the age of the child, if others were involved, and whether or not the child disclosed the abuse and how it was handled. Each person is different. Each situation is different.

Some trends have appeared, though.
For example:
- Psychological effects of child sexual abuse are usually greater when the abuse has involved physical violence.
- The psychological distress is usually greater if the child was abused by a trusted person rather than a stranger.
- Brief incidents of child sexual abuse usually have less of an impact than abuse that continues over a long period of time.
- Children abused when they are very young usually show fewer psychological effects than children who are abused when they are older.

How the Child Forms

The child within forms because the abused child is unable to handle emotions like an adult can. Although the child may feel the abuse is wrong, a young child gets very confused because the perpetrators enforce the notion that what happens is right. Plus, the child is usually rewarded for all the actions. Because they get so confused about it all, abused children lock the emotions deep inside. It's somewhat like forming a child within a child. In the end, the abuse may have caused them to feel guilt and shame, as well as anger and fear.

Sometimes a child who is being abused may tell somebody about what is happening. But many times, the older person she tells either refuses to believe her or doesn't want to get involved. If a child tells the mother, the mother will sometimes blame the child for what is happening. Other times, the mother tries to stop the abuse but finds out she can't without letting other people know. She may choose to do nothing because she's ashamed or doesn't want to break up the family.

Children who are sexually abused are usually afraid because the perpetrator may have made threats or the child feels nobody will believe her. The child may also be afraid the family will break up if she tells about the abuse. She may be afraid of losing the love, friendship or security of the abuser. The child who is a victim of abuse may also feel shame that other people will find out what happened. The child may think that people will regard her as dirty or bad if she tells.

Guilt is also common among abused children. The child may feel it's her fault, especially if she was rewarded for her actions. She may feel she is betraying the abuser if she tells on him. The child may also carry guilt because she may think she could have done something to stop the abuse.

Because of their age and inexperience in life, children don't have the capacity to cope with the feelings which overwhelm them as a result of abuse. So, when a child gets overwhelmed with emotions, the child shuts out those feelings, instead of letting them out in a healthy manner like an adult. The feelings go deeper inside the child, where they churn around for years on end. That bottled-up anger and frustration affects the child's emotional development. In later years, it's like having a child's emotions locked inside an adult's body.

The survivor might feel angry at the perpetrator for putting her through the abuse. She may also be angry at herself for letting it happen. She could carry a lot of anger towards her parents for not stopping the abuse. She may just be angry at anybody and everybody for what happened.

What About Me?

Dissociation

Children often lack the skills to objectively assess what they're learning. If they get mixed-up messages as a child, they are unable to determine what is right and wrong as an adult. Although a child may have sensed that the abuse which took place was wrong, the child doesn't know any different or how to avoid it. When a child is being abused by someone that she is supposed to respect and listen to, she tells herself: "I know this is wrong and I hate this feeling, but he is telling me that I have to do it."

Often the only way for a child to hang on is to dissociate herself from the abuse. The dissociation results in a child self being formed inside the subconscious of the survivor. The abuse may stop and the child may grow up, but the child within does not. All the thoughts and feelings that were there during the abusive years are still inside the person. So, if the abuse took place twenty years ago, the survivor has been carrying around those thoughts and feelings for twenty years.

The child may use a number of methods to dissociate herself from the abuse. In Liz's case, she used music. She remembers disco music playing when the abuse took place. She would focus on the disco music as a way of dissociating herself from what was happening to her body.

This dissociation can manifest itself in a number of ways later in life. I remember one day shopping with Liz. She insisted that we get a disco tape. It sounds silly, but since I wasn't a big disco fan, I questioned why it was so important. Well, I got my answer when she stormed out of the store in anger. I didn't know what I had said or done that had made her so mad. Later, when we visited our counselor, we explained what had happened and she pinned it down to the fact that the disco tape was important to the child within Liz because it was her only way of dissociating from abuse.

Survivors cope with the abuse and adjust to its effects in different ways. But ignoring the situation and hoping it will go away usually ends up backfiring. All the negative things that got locked away when the survivor was a child eventually come up in some way. And they can be triggered by a number of things.

76

An adult survivor of abuse may end up with a deep lack of trust for everyone, low self-esteem, depression, sexual and parenting problems. The survivor can also have memory blocks concerning their childhood years, recurring depression and suicidal tendencies. They may also have their feelings completely shut down, shut off or made inaccessible to anyone. Sometimes the survivor dissociates herself from any stressful situation or perceives the adult self and child self as two separate individuals.

As an adult, feelings of self-hatred, guilt or shame may lead to high-risk activities such as alcoholism, drug addiction or sexual promiscuity. One common symptom among survivors is eating disorders. In a 1990 study of 158 women with eating disorders, more than half divulged they had suffered some form of earlier sexual trauma.

Sometimes survivors don't manifest symptoms until they marry or have children. Occasionally, powerful, overwhelming feelings may arise from sexual activity or activities like diapering a helpless baby.

It is important that the survivor learn how to talk to the child within. A good professional counselor should be able to help the survivor get in touch with her inner self. The counselor will also be able to help the survivor manage, and cope with, this new-found entity.

It's equally important that you also learn how to cope with the child within. Rest assured, it is not something the survivor is making up. It is best if you accept the fact that the child exists and help the survivor learn how to handle it. Sometimes it could mean leaving the survivor alone for periods of time when she decides to deal with the child. Remember, the child is like any child. It wants attention and it wants to be assured it is safe. At times, the child will demand the survivor's complete attention, and that's when your feelings will just have to take a back seat for the time being.

You can slowly establish a relationship with the child too, although this can be a bit tricky. The child probably doesn't trust anyone, especially males, so don't expect immediate success with this approach. Patience is a virtue here. If you feel you aren't able to handle the whole episode of talking to the child within, don't try.

What About Me?

It's best not to offend the child and have to start from scratch again. It all sounds rather strange. But, when you're talking to the child within, what you're actually doing is talking to the survivor. The survivor may say things like "The little girl doesn't like men. She doesn't trust them." You may want to respond with something like this: "Well, she's right to think like that. She's been abused. But all men aren't like the one who abused her." Remember, trust has to be earned. The child within doesn't trust easily, and it's going to take a lot for you to earn her trust. Remember, the child within has been abused, so don't expect miracles too fast.

If you're trying to talk to the little girl and you don't know the answer to something, don't try to bluff her. It's best to let her know that you don't know something and be honest with her. She'll respect honesty. Never try to trick the little girl. She'll be too quick for that, and when she finds out, it will take a long time for her to trust you again.

Think of the child within as a real child and treat her with that same respect. Assure her that you'll protect her, that you'll try to help her and that you'll never give up on her. Don't yell at her if you get mad, because she'll just disappear and not come back for quite some time. Assure the child that you do believe her, that the abuse wasn't her fault and that you're not angry at her for it.

It doesn't happen all the time, but the child within usually disappears as the healing process nears an end. There's no time limit on all of this. Like the other parts of the healing process, it doesn't happen overnight. In the majority of cases, the adult and child become one. That's because, as a survivor heals, the child's emotions will heal too. In the end, the child no longer exists.

Points to Remember

- Children dissociate themselves from abuse.
- The child within is real.
- The child acts and feels like a real child.
- Learn to accept the child within.
- The child within usually disappears.

Chapter Eight
The Myths

Friends will ask. Family will ask. Even workmates will ask. In fact, so many people will ask that you'll probably get tired of hearing them ask. But the questions are unavoidable.

They'll want to know what's going on with the survivor, why she has to keep bringing up the sexual abuse which occurred in her past, why she can't just let it go and why she's putting you through all the agony as well. Usually, they're not mean-spirited about it all. They just don't understand what's involved and why it's so important for the survivor to heal.

You might as well get used to it. If they haven't hit you with these questions yet, you can bet they will soon. So you'd better get ready. The best way to be prepared is to educate yourself about the abuse so that you have some answers when the questions start coming.

Also, the more you understand, the more you're prepared for the rocky road which lies ahead. The more you learn about the survivor's healing process and everything else it entails, the less you will misjudge her, the fewer mistakes you'll make and the more you'll be able to help, rather than hinder, her healing from the past.

People are usually more curious than anything else when they ask about the problems you're facing. Usually they just don't know what's involved in the healing process or why it's so important to heal. By asking questions, they gain a better understanding of the problem and come to appreciate the magnitude of the healing process.

Most people aren't aware that childhood sexual abuse is one of the most devastating things that can happen to someone. They aren't aware of the long-term effects it can have on a person's life. They aren't aware that it robs its victims of their innocence, trust and self-esteem. Most people aren't aware that it introduces a child to adult sexuality before they're able to deal with it, that the memories can fester inside a survivor and create a lot of self-hate. They aren't aware it can, in many cases, cause self-destructive behavior in the survivor if she doesn't let it out, if she doesn't get help for the problem.

The Reactions You'll Get

Friends and family can be among the worst people to try and deal with, because they are usually more familiar with your personal situation than mere acquaintances and co-workers. If they underestimate the importance of the healing or fail to understand how deep the emotional scars can be, they can, in simple terms, be a pain in the butt.

I remember how my parents reacted. They didn't understand what Liz and I were going through. I asked them to be patient, but they still questioned why she had to confront the past. It was difficult to make them see why it was so important for her to heal. Every time I talked to them, they would ask what was going on, why I chose to go through this with Liz. In the end, after Liz had gone through her healing, I think they realized why it was so important to us.

Sometimes you might want to lash out at the world for failing to understand the predicament you're in. You might wonder why people keep pestering you with questions when you've already made it clear that the survivor is doing her best to heal from the abuse. Yet you can't blame people for their lack of understanding about the issue. After all, the sexual abuse of children is something that society has only recently come to terms with.

Yes, it's true that the problem has been around for centuries, but it's only in recent years that people have chosen to face up to the issue and its devastating effects. Only in recent years, with more and more women coming forward to tell their tales, has the crime been addressed at all.

Until recently, it has been dealt with behind closed doors, kept hidden by both survivors and their families. It's always been something that happens but is seldom discussed. So don't be alarmed when people ask questions and pester you about what's happening.

To understand more, just think back to when you were first asked to come to grips with the issue. Chances are you were a bit naive yourself. It's not surprising that people are in the dark about childhood sexual abuse. People have only been able to learn about the issue through television documentaries and movies. The media is a great way of providing information to the public, but in doing so, events are dramatized, and in some cases the public sees the issue through rose-colored glasses. It's little wonder, then, that there are a lot of myths and misconceptions about the problem. It's also little wonder that people have a lot of questions which still need answering.

More education about the problem is the only way that people will understand. It's the only way to debunk some of the myths and misconceptions that are out there. You can do your part by getting more information about child sexual abuse and increasing your knowledge of the issue. Not only will it help you deal with the survivor and understand her better, it will also help you to educate others.

So, just to get you ready, here are some of the common statements you might hear.

It was her fault too. She probably asked for it.

Nothing could be further from the truth. Keep in mind that the survivor was an innocent child, not a consenting adult, when the abuse occurred. She knew nothing about sex. She might have felt that what she was doing was wrong, but she didn't know how to prevent it. She was merely following the orders of an adult who was in a position of trust.

The abused child didn't know any better, but the adult did. Don't forget the child is truly the victim here and what the perpetrator did was a criminal act. Children never ask to be sexually abused.

She should be leaving the past alone. It all happened so long ago.

What About Me?

Should the person who has taken away the survivor's childhood go unpunished? Should that person be allowed to be free to do it again to some other vulnerable and unsuspecting child? Should that person be allowed to live his life without being held accountable for his actions?

It's true that many survivors don't care about the perpetrator and what becomes of him. Others, however, feel it is necessary that the perpetrator be held accountable and punished for his actions.

Sometimes it's just part of the healing process for the survivor. Other times, it's to stop a perpetrator from harassing the survivor or to prevent him from harming another child.

Whatever the reason, it's important the survivor deal with her past to get on with her future. Nobody can tell the survivor she shouldn't deal with the past.

She should have told someone about it.

Many times young children who are abused do tell someone about it. But many times they aren't believed or nobody wants to stand up to the perpetrator. Sometimes abused children don't say anything because they're so afraid of what the perpetrator will do to them. Other times, they don't tell because the perpetrator is someone they are supposed to trust and they don't want him to get in trouble.

Abused children are often confused about what's happening. It may feel wrong, but they're often rewarded by the perpetrator for doing it. The point is that no child deserves to be abused, and whether the child did or didn't say anything about it makes no difference at all. Remember, it's not up to the children to do something about the problem of abuse. It's everybody's responsibility.

It wasn't really abuse because it happened only a few times.

How many times have you heard this one? But abuse is abuse no matter how many times it occurs. The act of sexually abusing a young child is still a criminal one even if it happened only once.

A child who is abused once may not be as affected as a child who was abused repeatedly, but that doesn't change the nature of the crime. When a child is abused, the child is abused. It affects each one in some way. The number of times it occurred has no bearing on whether it was abuse. If it happened once, twice or twenty times, it was still abuse.

It didn't cause any damage because she looks fine.

The survivor may appear fine on the outside, but her emotions may be in shambles. The abuse may have taken its toll on the inside. The distress may range from mild to severe, depending on the circumstances of the abuse. If it was brief and short-lived, the effects may not be as severe. If the abuse took place over a long period of time, however, the effects will probably be much more severe. Much depends on the severity of the abuse and whether it involved fondling or intercourse.

Survivors of childhood sexual abuse are often very good at hiding their real feelings from people and they appear fine on the outside. It's what they've been used to doing all their lives. But don't underestimate how devastating childhood sexual abuse can be.

She's always got a problem. She always has to be the center of attention.

Yes, she does have problems. And yes, she may always want attention. But there's probably a good reason for it—the abuse. She may always be seeking to be the life of the party because she's been abused and didn't have a chance at any normal kind of emotional development.

The adult survivor of child abuse may have a totally different outlook on life than most people. She may want the attention because she thinks it's the only way people will like her. Instead of criticizing someone for these types of actions, perhaps it is wiser to get to the root of the problem, find out why they act that way, and then try to help them.

What About Me?

It can't be her father. He loves her. Besides, he's a respected man in the community.

All the more reason to suspect him, because most perpetrators are known to the child. They're usually a person in a position of trust, someone she believes in and respects. The perpetrator often gets away with it while the child is still young because he can still use his position of trust and power to do harm to the young child.

About one in four assailants is a family member or a person in a position of trust. About half of the assailants are friends or acquaintances of the child. Only about one in six is a stranger. It is much rarer to find that the perpetrator didn't know the child.

Doubters Will Always Exist

There will always be people who doubt that child sexual abuse really does exist, so you're not going to win everybody over. Even telling people the facts isn't going to convince all of them. Some people just refuse to admit it happens. Others feel it shouldn't be talked about. They feel it should be kept within the family. Still others believe it's not really a serious problem in society.

Usually, it's that lack of education about the problem that is responsible for these feelings. If people knew more about the devastating effects that childhood sexual abuse can have on a person, they might not be so quick to deny its existence. They might have more intense feelings about the issue. If they knew more about the serious social consequences, they might want to learn more. In the end, all of society would benefit.

You can't blame people for their ignorance, though. Unless you're involved in something there isn't much need to learn about it, is there? You might not know a lot about alcoholism or drug abuse, but you can bet that someone who has a partner who is an alcoholic or drug abuser knows a lot about the problem and the issue. It's just human nature not to worry about things that don't affect you.

But you're reading this book because you have an interest in childhood sexual abuse. It likely affects you and now you're forced to deal with it—to look it squarely in the face and fight. You probably wouldn't be interested in reading about childhood sexual abuse if it hadn't reared its ugly head in your life. If your wife didn't have to deal with the effects of it, you might never have worried about it at all, right?

Don't be taken aback at how naive people may be about the subject. And don't get too upset at some of their questions or the statements they make. The best approach to the whole problem is to treat it as a learning experience. The more knowledge you can pass on to somebody else, the better. When people begin to understand more about the issue, about what you and the survivor are going through and what they can do to help you, their support can be invaluable.

If you can just win over one supporter, the world will be better off than it was before, because those supporters, like yourself, will now be on the lookout for such abuse. You'll also have extra support—something you might need in the long run.

Points to Remember

- Many people don't understand the effects of childhood sexual abuse.
- Don't blame people for their lack of knowledge about the subject.
- Do your best to educate others about the issue.
- You won't win everybody over.

Chapter Nine
The Confrontation

At some point, it could very well happen.

The survivor may want to confront the perpetrator and anyone else who let the abuse happen—friends, family and relatives included.

She may want to set the record straight, let everybody know who abused her and make it clear that she's not going to take it from the perpetrator any more. She may want to let the whole world in on the secret. She may want everybody to know what happened to her.

For you, this is going to be a real eye-opener. It may also be an especially difficult period if you've known the perpetrator for years and have a relationship with him and the survivor's family. The prospect of suddenly being in a face-to-face confrontation with him doesn't sound too appealing. But there's no use beating around the bush here. Some things you just have to do. There are times when you just have to grin and bear it, and this happens to be one of those times. It's for the betterment of both of you.

Think about it for a moment. You don't want to be hanging around with a guy who molests little girls, do you? You don't want your wife or partner hanging around someone who molested her as a child, do you? You don't want other innocent children falling prey to the same abuse, do you?

Experts say not all survivors will want to confront the perpetrator. It depends on the survivor. Sometimes survivors will feel sorry for the perpetrator or they may not want to upset the family. It's an important step in the healing process, however, and you should support the survivor if she does choose to confront the perpetrator.

All this shouldn't come as a total surprise to you. You've probably thought about the problem at times during the healing process. You must have thought there would come a time when the survivor might want the perpetrator to face the music. You must have thought how it would happen, how the survivor would tell him, how she might want to set the record straight and how you would cope.

If, by some strange reason you haven't, though, you might want to put this book down for a moment and give it some thought right now.

It's a progressive step if the survivor wants to take the perpetrator to task. The reasons may vary, but many survivors feel it's something they have to do in order to protect other children. People will be more reluctant to let their children hang around a man who's been called a perpetrator, right?

There's another reason, though. Exposing the perpetrator also places the blame where it should lie—squarely on the shoulders of the perpetrator. For years the survivor has probably been carrying around shame, guilt and a lot of anger. Exposing the perpetrator shifts that burden. No longer is the problem hidden. The perpetrator—as the survivor did for so many years—will have to live with a cloud hanging over him.

In Liz's case, she exposed the perpetrator—her stepfather—not only for herself, but also to protect her nieces and nephews. She confronted her stepfather directly one day when he came to pick up her mother at work. She had been working with her mother and when he came into the room she met him face to face. She told him she was well aware of what he did to her as a child, she told him she wasn't afraid of him any more and that he would pay for what he did. She yelled at him, screamed at him and told him never to come near her again. Then she left.

Don't Worry

Don't get afraid and all tied up in knots when the survivor tells you she wants to confront the perpetrator. Again, like the other steps in the healing process, it is a big step in the right direction.

After all, isn't it time the perpetrator paid for taking from the life of the survivor? Isn't it time he felt some of the things the survivor has carried around with her all these years? Isn't it time he felt ashamed, guilty and angry, like the survivor has felt all these

What About Me?

years? Isn't it time he was made accountable for what he has taken? The survivor isn't taking a step backwards by confronting the perpetrator. By doing it she's progressing. When the survivor wants to confront the perpetrator, she's doing it because she's decided it's something she wants to do. It's much different than being angry. So if the survivor tells you she wants to confront the perpetrator, you can bet she really means it. Don't try to stop her. Just help her do it in the right way.

Basically, there are two ways the survivor can confront the perpetrator—directly or indirectly. The circumstances of the abuse and the perpetrator's temperament and disposition will factor greatly into this. So will the attitudes of the survivor towards the perpetrator and her reasons for exposing him.

If the perpetrator is a violent person and likely to bring harm to the survivor or her family, she may prefer to expose him indirectly. If she's still afraid of confronting him face to face, she may want to phone him, write him a letter or send a tape-recorded message to him. She's still getting the message across—it's just that she's doing it in the way that she feels most comfortable.

The direct approach may be used by the survivor if she feels she has healed and is strong enough to cope with the anger of the perpetrator or whatever other problems he may try and cause her. It also depends a lot on how much support the survivor has. If she has little support, she may doubt herself and have difficulty confronting the perpetrator. With a lot of support, though, she'll feel positive about what she's doing and do it in a strong, confident manner.

Let Her Decide

Whatever approach the survivor decides to take, it is important that you let her make the decision. You'll just have to accept her judgment here. Remember, she's doing this for herself and her healing. It's very important that she empower herself to do it the way that she wants to do it.

Sure, you may have a very strong desire to confront the perpe-

88

trator for her. You might want to wring his neck for her, say a few choice words to him, let him know what you think of him. You have a right to feel this way. After all, what is happening affects you too. However, this isn't your fight. It's the survivor's, and it's up to her how she wants to deal with the perpetrator.

Liz and I lived in a small city and every time I saw her stepfather the anger would boil inside me. He'd go out of his way to make sure I saw him. Some mornings, he'd sit in his truck outside of where I worked, just so I knew he was around. I wanted to grab him and belt him silly for what he had done, but I didn't because I knew it wouldn't help Liz in her healing. It's one of the most difficult things I've ever had to do, but I did manage to restrain myself. I just wanted to give him one good shot, but I held myself back.

Looking back now, I realize I did the right thing by restraining myself. It might have brought some immediate satisfaction, but it wouldn't have done Liz or me any good in the long run. I would have ended up in jail and she would have ended up worrying about me.

It's tough, but you have to hold back. You have to let the survivor determine how she wants to deal with the perpetrator. It wouldn't be fair to take that away from her, would it? It's better if she decides how she'll deal with him. It's better if she decides how she's going to do it and where she's going to do it. You may have some strong views on how all this should be done, but for the time being, it's wise to keep them to yourself.

It will work out for the better if you let the survivor sort things out here. She's got a lot on her plate and she doesn't need the extra burden of worrying about your thoughts and feelings. But, that doesn't mean you can't be a help to her. You can have some input and you can encourage her to confront the perpetrator using the right method and manner. You could sit and plan it all with her, giving her the final say in all decisions, of course.

Whether she chooses the direct or indirect approach, there are a few things which should be worked out beforehand. If she chooses the direct approach, it's probably not a bad idea for her to rehearse how she's going to go about confronting the perpetrator.

What About Me?

You could help by setting up the scenario, encouraging her to practice and helping her find the courage within herself to carry it through.

After all, she'll want to say all she has to say in the short time period she has to say it. She won't want to miss anything because it's probably a one-shot deal. You can help her rehearse how she's going to do it.

For example, make sure she answers these simple questions:

What happened? It's better if the survivor tells the perpetrator in no uncertain terms exactly what happened and why she is talking to him.

How has it affected her? The survivor must make clear what the abuse has done to her and how it has taken away from her life and person.

How does she feel about the perpetrator? It's important that the survivor leave no doubt in the perpetrator's mind what she thinks about the abuse and him.

Stay Alert

Once the perpetrator has been told what the score is, don't let your guard down. You need to be ready for anything. A lot of things happen within families once the situation is confronted and out in the open. A lot of emotions are stirred up. A lot of feelings are exposed.

Sometimes the perpetrator will let the situation ride, but not often. The perpetrator may hope that nothing more will come of it. He may try to distance the survivor from the family so others won't get on the bandwagon. Other times, the perpetrator will fight back with more abuse—trying to show the survivor that more harm will come to her if she tells, just as he may have done when the survivor was a child.

In our case, Liz's stepfather tried everything he could to harass us. He had her mother phone our house. He even phoned my workplace and told people I was trying to hurt him. The day before he was to be sentenced in court on charges of molesting Liz as a child, he tried cutting her off in her car and threatened to kill her.

There was one time that I nearly lost my cool with him. I was in the grocery store and I saw him standing and sneering at me from a few feet away. I decided I wasn't going to take it any more and called his bluff. I faced him and called him a child molester in front of all the people in the store. He left and told the police I had threatened to kill him. However, before I had approached him I had asked one of the stockboys in the store to listen to what I was going to say to the perpetrator. Luckily, I had protected myself.

Don't Take It on Yourself

There are a number of ways to deal with a perpetrator who does cross the line, and we'll deal with that in more detail in the next chapter. Suffice it to say, the best way to deal with a problem perpetrator is through the legal system. By letting authorities handle a problem situation, you don't get personally involved and go and do something stupid that will hamper the survivor's healing process.

Remember, a lot of tensions and emotions are running high at this time. The perpetrator is being made accountable for something he never thought he'd be held accountable for. You're involved in something you likely never thought would happen to you. It's easy to step over the boundary and get yourself in real deep trouble by bopping the perpetrator and feeling better about yourself. But getting yourself into trouble won't help the survivor progress in her healing, and that is what is most important.

The moral in all of this is to leave it up to the authorities to handle. That way you don't get personally involved. That way you don't get in any trouble.

Unfortunately, it sounds as if what you have to do here is sit back and watch. To some extent, that seems to be right. You have to let the survivor confront the perpetrator in the manner she wants to. But you also have to be there—ready and willing—when she calls on you for support, help or understanding. That's how you're involved.

You have to show a lot of compassion here. You have to put your feelings about all this in your pocket for the time being and let the survivor get hers dealt with. If you have too much trouble with your anger and frustration about this whole thing, perhaps you should see a counselor yourself to help release those frustrations in a positive manner. It won't do any good venting them on the survivor. She has enough to cope with just now.

All this might seem like a pretty tall order. But it'll be worth it down the road when you see the survivor healing and the perpetrator still carrying guilt.

I used to get angry when I saw the perpetrator. He'd walk down the street like he didn't have a care in the world. It bothered me then because Liz was still suffering from the abuse he caused. But now that Liz has healed, it doesn't bother me. He's still living in a miserable world. He was taken to task for his actions and he no longer has any control over her.

Be Cautious

It's so important to let the survivor confront the perpetrator in her own way. The survivor will build self-esteem and feel better about herself if she is able to confront the perpetrator on her own. The important thing is to be supportive of the survivor.

Don't be afraid or embarrassed about seeking professional counseling for yourself. You're dealing with a very emotionally charged issue here and it's important for you to deal with your feelings in a constructive manner. You don't want to be bogging the survivor down with your feelings. Right now it's the survivor's fight. She needs to say what she has to say. Remember, it's not your turn yet. It may never be your turn. So if you have to express your anger, you have to do it in another way.

Hitting a punching bag with the perpetrator's face on it is constructive. You're venting your anger, but not damaging the healing of the survivor. And you're getting a good workout in the process. Writing a letter, making a tape, yelling in a closed room, or group counseling sessions are great ways of getting rid of the anger and frustration. There are other, more productive ways to vent your anger. Perhaps working towards tougher laws for child abusers would help alleviate some of the anger that you might have built up.

Once the survivor has confronted the perpetrator, you'll probably feel a sense of relief. The survivor, on the other hand, will feel a lot of satisfaction. The survivor may also have a great feeling of empowerment and want to change other things about her life. She's lifted a heavy burden from her shoulders. She's confronted the person who took so much away from her, the person she couldn't confront as a helpless child. Imagine how uplifting that is for her.

Just a word of warning here, though. This uplifting feeling of empowerment over her life may now be tested in other areas. As she gains the self-confidence to confront her past, you might also find yourself on the hit list.

She may want to change some of the things about you that are bothering her. So you might want to keep on your toes at this stage. You could also become the target of her new-found empowerment. You could become the subject of her scrutiny as she examines the rest of her life and decides whether anything needs changing.

Now, just because she may want some changes doesn't mean she doesn't like you or want you around. It just means there may be some things you do which bother her but she's never had the courage to speak up before. Now she has that courage and wants something done.

Keep an open mind here. Sure, there are certain things you might not want to change, so discuss it with her. She'll realize you still have to be the person you are, but don't balk at her suggestions. They might be very reasonable. They might, in fact, make you a better person.

Points to Remember

- The survivor might want to confront the perpetrator.
- Confronting the perpetrator is a good move for her.
- The confrontation can be direct or indirect.
- Help her do it in the proper manner.
- Let police handle any fallout.

Chapter Ten
The Aftermath

Okay, it's done.

The perpetrator has been exposed. The cat's out of the bag. Now what?

Well, buckle up and get ready for some real action over the next few weeks. The Hatfields and the McCoys were nothing compared to what can happen when a perpetrator is exposed. Once that happens you can expect all hell to break loose. Family members might take sides. The battle lines might get drawn between the survivor and the family. After that, the denials, accusations and stories might really start to fly.

The perpetrator will probably deny it: "I never did anything wrong," he will say. "It's all in her head. She's lying. She's just trying to cause a family rift."

The mother will probably defend him: "Oh, she's always been a little strange," she'll say. "I don't know what's wrong with her. She'll get over it in time, I'm sure."

Siblings will probably side-step the issue: "Nothing happened to me," they'll say. "I don't remember anything. He wasn't a bad guy."

In all of this confusion, however, there's one thing you can bet on—the survivor is the only one telling the truth about what really happened. Her story is the only one you can truly believe. Everybody will deny there's a problem while the survivor faces up to it.

It's simple to see why. There's nothing pretty about child abuse, and families don't want to admit when it does happen. It's embarrassing to families. It can rip them apart at the seams once they're exposed, so in many cases families will do all they can to keep it quiet.

It doesn't happen in every case, but when a survivor exposes the problem she's often ostracized by her family. She might be left alone to deal with the emotional scars of the abuse. Others in the family might not have faced up to the fact the abuse occurred or they may just want to keep it hidden. The survivor might not fit in with the family any more. She may be creating too many ripples in the pond. Therefore, she gets banished from the family for speaking about it. She's labeled a problem child, someone who is always stirring up trouble. Meanwhile, the rest of the family—the perpetrator, the mother, the other siblings—bond closer to try to secure what they have left.

It can be a particularly painful time for the survivor. Not only is she trying to deal with the emotional pain of facing up to the abuse, but she is also dealing with alienation from her family. It's all very confusing because she has a lot of good reasons for confronting the situation but she probably also has a lot of memories of good times with her family. Although there was abuse, she may still have warm memories of times like Christmases and birthdays.

In our case, Liz knew the situation had to be confronted, but she was still sad because there had also been good times with her family. It was a very emotional experience for her, having to separate the good from the bad. It took her years to figure out which parts of her past she wanted to remember fondly and which parts of her past she wanted to discard. Christmas is still a tough time for her because it is a time when so much emphasis is placed upon the family. Because she doesn't have a family now, it is particularly difficult for her to be upbeat about the festive season. Time is healing the wounds, however, and as each Christmas passes it gets easier for her.

Salvaging the Good

Once the survivor has exposed the truth, she'll still attempt to salvage some good from the bad. Even in the most dysfunctional of families there is still some good mixed in with the bad. She'll have to decide what can be salvaged from her family and what needs to be discarded. It becomes very confusing for her to sort out the good from the bad and she needs time to do this.

As a supporter, all you can do is provide a listening ear and let her know she still has someone who believes her and does care. It

may take the survivor some time, perhaps even years, to decide
how she wants to deal with the rest of the family, with her brothers
and sisters who might maintain the abuse didn't occur or aren't
ready to speak about it. But she'll do it.

In Liz's case, the decisions were made fairly quickly—over a
period of months. Nobody supported her when she made the decision to confront the perpetrator. Her mother, a brother and a sister
all wondered why she had to do such a thing. They all stuck by
the perpetrator.

Months later, Liz did talk to her brother and sister to see if
there was a chance a relationship could be worked out, but it was
her own decision that none could. She told each of them that she
was unable to see them any more because they still associated with
the perpetrator and hadn't acknowledged what he had done. It was
a painful process for her, but also necessary if she was to live a life
free from the abuse.

Sorting out family ties is a difficult process for the survivor. She
may approach family members many times as she heals to see if
they'll come over to her side. There's no harm in all of this if she's
healed enough. Once she is well on the road to recovery, she'll
never be able to go back to abuse. So don't worry about her slipping
back into the folds of an abusive situation and falling prey to the
very people who abused her in the first place. It just won't happen.

When she reaches out to her family, all she's doing is extend-
ing the olive branch to see if any of the family members who may
have been abused or didn't believe her at first will reach out for
that branch and join her in healing from the past. If she's healed,
there's no harm in trying. In fact, she may do some good. Perhaps
another family member who was abused by the same perpetrator
might have been too afraid in the beginning to come forward.
Perhaps that family member wanted to make the break but just
didn't know how.

The survivor shouldn't put all her eggs in one basket, though.
It might not work out. In fact, in most cases it does not. The survivor has to be ready for a lot of disappointment here. Many times,
families in which abuse occurred become so close-knit that even
the truth won't cause the members to separate from the perpetrator.

Testing the Family

The survivor will probably want to test each member of her family individually, so be prepared for a lot of ups and downs during this tumultuous period of her healing. She'll want to explore what type of relationship, if any, she can have with each individual member of her family. She may have vowed many times in the past that she'd never talk to any of them again, but chances are she'll try to keep the lines of communication open to see if any of them have changed their minds. If they haven't, you can rest assured she'll figure it out quickly, more quickly than she has in the past, and not bother with them again.

It's easy to see why the survivor wants to help other members of her family. As she heals, she begins to experience what life is like without the shame, anger and guilt many abused children feel years later. She's realized the gains she's made from her healing and she only wants the others to realize the benefits as well. Unfortunately, all members of a family aren't as receptive to the offers. Many family members will turn their backs on the survivor or just lead her on.

It's difficult to watch the survivor go through this process. She will have a lot of headaches and heartaches as she tries to determine which family members she can trust and have relationships with. But, like the other stages of healing, it is an essential one to go through.

How close the survivor remains to her family is something only she can decide. There are a lot of variables at work here—like whether the family is prepared to admit the truth or whether they care about the truth. The more the survivor heals, the more easily she'll be able to figure them out, and the less time she'll spend trying to get help for someone who doesn't really want to be helped.

Setting Boundaries

She may go about testing the boundaries with her family in different ways. She may opt to have a temporary separation from her family in order to work out her feelings and see if she wants a relationship with anybody. She may want to heal further so she is stronger to deal with the family. She may also impose a cooling-off period.

When Liz decided to deal with her family, it was quick and deliberate. She gave them a chance to see her point of view, and when they refused to confront the situation, she decided not to have contact with any of them. I think it helped her recover much faster. Because there was no tugging at the heartstrings, Liz healed more quickly than a lot of survivors. By separating from her family, she didn't have to deal with a lot of the emotional upheaval that accompanies a perpetrator's being exposed. She didn't have to be a part of the bickering and side-taking that goes on when a perpetrator is exposed.

That's not to say that everything was a bed of roses for us. Liz still had her problems. In addition to healing, she had to come to grips with the fact that her family didn't support her and what she was doing. That in itself was an emotional nightmare. But she did come to grips with it and sort through the process by herself.

Each situation and each family is different, but if the survivor feels her recovery is thwarted by the family, then she will have little other choice than to pull away from them—at least temporarily. In many cases, complete separation is the only answer.

A survivor might want to separate from the family if:
- She finds that the family continually denies the abuse took place and isn't willing to get help.
- The family continues to try and abuse the survivor.
- The family continually upsets her and generally won't let her live a normal life.
- The family is also dysfunctional in other ways.
- The family tells the survivor that she shouldn't deal with her past and attempts to interfere with her recovery.
- The perpetrator doesn't get any help for his problem.

Sometime during the healing process, the survivor will have to deal with her family. The survivor has to work out the past, and determine who she can trust and not trust, before she can move ahead with her healing. She might also decide to take legal action against the perpetrator, for a number of reasons. She may just want him to pay for what he did to her. She might want to protect other children from the perpetrator. Whatever the reason, she has every right to take legal action because what the perpetrator did was a crime.

In most countries, the legal system is fairly open when it comes to the length of time the survivor can wait before deciding to charge a perpetrator in court. It's not uncommon for perpetrators to be sent to jail two decades after the abuse occurred.

That's exactly what happened in our case. Liz took her stepfather to court more than twenty years after the abuse occurred, and he was sentenced to a three-month jail term. He later spent another day in jail for threatening to kill her. Although it took a lot of time and patience, not to mention a lot of police work, the rewards were well worth it. After the conviction, Liz felt a relief that the courts had finally believed what she knew to be the case. She also knew that he could no longer deny his actions—and be believed.

Relations May Get Worse

Once a survivor has decided to charge the perpetrator relations with the survivor's family can only get worse, especially if nobody else is admitting the abuse occurred. Families will do just about anything to make sure the survivor doesn't cause any problems for them. First, they may deny there ever was a problem. Then, they may try to coax the survivor into keeping the problem quiet. Lastly, they'll threaten her—especially if charges are considered. They don't have a lot to lose, and perpetrators are so used to being in control they'll resort to just about anything to stop from being exposed.

Now this is where you come in—big time. Throughout this book you've been told, in many cases, to relax, take it easy, not worry. Well, now you can do something you'll really feel good about. There's nothing that says a survivor has to put up with continual harassment from a perpetrator. She has a right to a safe, secure life. So do you.

If you find the perpetrator is causing problems for her—whether he's calling your house or sitting in a car outside her work—make problems for him. Just one word of caution, however. Make sure you do it legally, otherwise you won't be doing anybody any good.

Do it legally—but do something. You can protect the survivor and you can do it in the right manner without getting yourself in trouble. Don't forget, the important point here is not to get yourself in trouble. Nobody benefits if you go and threaten the perpetrator, punch him out and leave him bleeding in a ditch somewhere. Sure, it might make you feel better. But the only thing it will bring you, and the survivor, is grief and trouble—something she doesn't need any more of at this point in her healing.

You won't do the survivor any good if you're behind bars for punching out the perpetrator. A judge might think you had a good reason, but he'll still punish you because it's unacceptable behavior. It might help you let off some steam, but in the end it will only build more frustration. Court processes are long and strenuous, so don't cause yourself any more grief than you have to.

Remember, your job here is to help and protect the survivor, not to vent your frustrations by beating up on the perpetrator. Keep your cool and deal with the perpetrator in the proper manner. That means going to law enforcement authorities every time there's a problem. Don't try to handle it yourself because it will only backfire on you.

I think police in the city we lived in got tired of hearing from us. But every time I got a phone call from the perpetrator, every time I had tire marks on my front lawn or nails in my tire, they'd get a visit from Liz and me. We knew there wasn't anything they could do about many of these things, but we felt safer if they knew what was going on. There's no harm in letting police in on the situation. Remember, they're there to help. They don't like to see good people harassed.

Try not to beat the perpetrator at his own game. Don't get into a tit-for-tat exchange with him. It's better to let the police handle it. You'll only be playing his game if you try to deal with the perpetrator on your own. You'll end up playing on his turf. Remember, he's got nothing to lose and everything to gain by playing this way. Perpetrators are good at it. Police officers, on the other hand, are trained to handle these situations, so let them do their job.

Sometimes you may get frustrated with the efforts of the police. You might feel they're not doing enough to protect you from the perpetrator. Keep in mind, though, there's only so much they can do. They have their hands tied too. They have only so much authority. The law enforcement authorities will do what they can to help. If you're being harassed and they can do something about it, they will. The authorities don't like perpetrators any more than you do.

If you're at your wit's end and can't get any action from the police, there are other legal avenues to pursue. The laws vary from place to place, so it is best to contact a lawyer to see what you can do. In most places, legal consultation is free for the first half-hour so it may be well worth the time spent to seek a lawyer's advice. They can advise you on such things as peace bonds, restraining orders, trespassing notices and how to launch a civil lawsuit.

Yes, the period after a perpetrator is confronted can be a long, upsetting and frustrating time. But if you're patient, and deal with the family and the perpetrator in the proper manner, you'll come out a winner when the dust settles.

Points to Remember

- The survivor is often outcast by her family.
- The survivor will try to salvage some good from the bad.
- Relations with the family will probably get worse after the truth is out.
- Deal with any problems legally.

Chapter Eleven
Gaining Trust

It doesn't matter where you are.

You could be walking down the street, watching a movie or just plain stopped in a traffic jam cursing at the guy ahead with the broken-down car. You have to face it. You're always under the gun.

As the survivor heals, you can bet she'll be watching you like a hawk. She'll watch to see if you look at other women. She'll watch you when movie sex scenes are playing. She'll even snoop through your belongings and desk drawers to see if anything is out of the ordinary.

Sure, it's unsettling, but it isn't unusual for survivors of child sexual abuse.

For the time being, you'll just have to walk on eggshells—not knowing what might set her off. You see, what the survivor is trying to do is find out who she can and can't trust. The closer she gets to you, the more she'll question it. It's not surprising; trust is something she's never experienced in her life. The abuse she suffered as a child destroyed her ability to trust anyone. One of the people she trusted most in life was probably the one who abused her.

It all makes perfect sense if you think about it for a moment. When your first sexual experience as a child is abusive, it changes your outlook on trust. The survivor was never allowed to figure things out for herself, or experience normal sexual feelings through a normal series of life experiences. It was forced upon her in an ugly manner. She was never able to experience for herself what is and isn't trust. She wasn't allowed to make the necessary mistakes and implement the necessary checks and balances to find out for herself who you can and cannot trust in this world.

Because the survivor was abused, she had to learn quickly. She learned that even someone she loves cannot be trusted fully.

While most children are taught to watch out for the stranger, the person that might pull up alongside them in a car and attempt to abduct them, most aren't taught that the perpetrators can exist right in their own safe homes.

The effect of abuse can make itself felt in ways that you might not even have realized. When things are going well between the two of you, it might make the survivor uncomfortable. She might have to sabotage a good thing or even a relationship just to reinforce the notion that men can't be trusted. After all, a male figure the survivor trusted and looked up to as a child was probably the one who abused her. What kind of message does that send to a young child?

In the beginning, the relationship between Liz and me was very rocky for this very reason. We fell into a pattern. Things would be fine for a few weeks. Everything would be going really well. Then, all of a sudden, usually after a period of three weeks, we'd be getting too close and she would call the whole thing off. For no reason at all, she'd tell me it wasn't working out and she couldn't see me any more. It was downright confusing, not to mention infuriating.

It wasn't until later, when Liz and I went to a counselor, that I learned the real reason this was happening. She had a fear that bad followed good because the abuse by her stepfather always followed good times with him. He would suddenly turn around and abuse her. As a child, Liz got used to this cycle, so later in life, when things were going well between the two of us, she had to sabotage the relationship because she feared it would turn rotten anyway.

Trust

It's quite common for a perpetrator to be a person in a position of trust. That's how he's so successful in getting away with the hideous crime. The perpetrator either threatens the child so the child is too afraid to tell on him, or the perpetrator leads the child into thinking she is doing the right thing by not telling.

It's not surprising, then, that the adult survivor of childhood sexual abuse gets so confused when it comes to trusting someone. So, while you might be trying to do good things for the survivor, don't be surprised if she questions your motives. In her mind, it's possible that an abusive situation will follow the good times she's having with you.

As an adult, Liz had the toughest time trusting anyone—including me. It took years for me to earn her trust. She'd watch me closely, test me to see if I was telling the truth. One day we were shopping and I mentioned that she might look good in a certain dress. Well, that was the end of that. She wondered where I had got the idea she might look good in the dress. She wondered who I had seen it on before.

This lack of trust can manifest itself in a number of ways. For example, the survivor may have a tough time saying she loves you because that's what the perpetrator told her. To her, love is a dirty word. It's the same word she heard when bad things were happening to her. So you can't blame her now for not wanting to be loved, can you? In her way of thinking, she can't trust or love you because of that past.

Be Honest

It'll take time—a lot of time—for her to come to grips with the situation. The only way you can help is by being open and honest with her. The survivor will have to learn through experience and time—a long period of time—that you are much different from the perpetrator, that your thoughts and intentions are in no way like his.

At times, the survivor may even test your honesty. She'll ask you about stories you've told her in the past to see if the facts are still the same. Even a little white lie can upset the survivor a lot, so don't even try it. Remember, she already thinks all men lie. Once she catches you lying about something, she's confirmed her beliefs and it will take her a long time to trust you once again.

Honesty is your best policy here. Using your own common sense is another. Be honest with the survivor. Sit with her and talk about how you feel about the situation. Tell her your shortcomings. That way, if something does happen and you're in trouble, she knows you're not trying to abuse her. She knows it's something you can't help.

For example, some people have trouble making appointments on time. Some people won't fill up the gas tank in the car until it's on empty. If you've noticed these peculiarities about yourself, tell the survivor. That way when you don't show up right on the button, she understands it's not because of her. She'll realize it's a problem that you have. Also, when you run out of gas in the middle of nowhere, she won't think you planned it that way. That doesn't mean she still won't lambaste you for being a flaming idiot, but she won't think you're trying to abuse her as she was abused in the past.

It's important to talk with the survivor about your shortcomings. After all, nobody in this world can be expected to be 100 per cent trustworthy. It's just part of our nature to fail sometimes. We're all human. How many times have you said you'd be somewhere at a certain time and found yourself running late for no reason of your own? You see, you can't be perfect. So accept that fact. But do your best to be where you said you'd be and do what you said you'd do.

If you fail, tell the survivor why you failed. It's important she know the real reason. And she deserves an explanation. The last thing she deserves is to be disappointed, manipulated or lied to again.

Of course, the best way to build trust is to be trustworthy; that goes without saying. So now might be a good time to sit down and evaluate yourself to see how trustworthy you really are. Some of us think we're trustworthy, but when it gets right down to it, we fall short. The more trustworthy you are, the more the survivor will trust you. It all makes sense. The less trustworthy you are, the less she'll trust you.

Try this. Make up a list of the things you feel you can be trusted to do. Then make up a list which shows why you're unreliable. Which list is longer? What does that tell you? Once you've done the lists, see if you can make some improvements. Be honest with yourself when you do this.

What About Me?

Ask yourself some of these questions:

- Do I keep my promises?
- Do I tell little white lies to get what I want?
- Do I safeguard confidences?
- Would I make a trustworthy friend?
- Would I trust myself?

This isn't scientific and there's no perfect way to score this test. Only you can decide how trustworthy you are. Still, sitting down and compiling a list might help you to realize where your shortcomings are and where you can improve. At least this way, if your partner gets upset because you can't be relied on, you know exactly what she's talking about.

If, after making up the list, you're satisfied that you are a fairly trustworthy person, then you're in good shape. You've got a good base to start from. Barring a few minor problems, you should pull through all this okay. If you're not, however, you've got some work to do.

You're Not Superhuman

The survivor won't expect you to be superhuman. She'll realize that you can't be trustworthy all the time. But she will expect you to be trustworthy when it really counts.

It all sounds very stressful, and it is. Finding a way to cope under this ever-watchful eye can be a very difficult process indeed. But you can help minimize potentially explosive situations by avoiding them.

For example, don't go to movies where you're sure a sex scene is to be played out. Avoid watching television shows that exploit women. It only makes sense. The survivor is trying to heal from abuse and doesn't want to see a rape scene played out on the big screen in front of her with you eyeballing the movie and munching on some popcorn. Getting rid of any girlie magazines might also be a good idea for the same reason. The survivor is sensitive to anything that looks like exploitation or abuse. Now is probably a good time to stop ogling other women, too.

This whole process can be very frustrating, especially if you're a well-rounded character. You may have to take some lumps for things you didn't do. You may feel you shouldn't have to earn the survivor's trust, but you have to face the reality of the situation you are in. She was abused and trust for her is non-existent.

One thing's for certain about all this. If you pass the test, you will gain her trust. That's not to say things are going to be consistently rosy. But, if the survivor begins to show trust for you, it's going to make things a lot easier. And both of you will benefit from that.

Points to Remember

- A survivor finds it difficult to trust anyone.
- Earning her trust takes time.
- Expect to be tested.
- Honesty is your best policy.

Chapter Twelve
Nightmares

You've probably experienced it many times already. It's the middle of the night and you and the survivor are sleeping soundly. Suddenly, the peaceful silence is shattered. The survivor jerks herself upright in bed and sits there, staring with a look of horror into the darkness. She grabs you by the arm. Her frightened fingers tighten around your arm like a vice. Her eyes widen like saucers.

"Can you hear them?" she says in a quivering voice. "I can hear them. They're footsteps. Listen to them. He's coming after me."

As you try to collect your thoughts, the survivor is pushing you to investigate.

"Quick, he's coming up the stairs," she says. "Hurry, go and see if it's him."

The terror in her voice is contagious. Now you're scared stiff too. But like a flash you're out of bed, on your feet and heading towards the door. Then it hits you. Wait a minute, you didn't hear anything at all. You didn't hear any footsteps, noises or anybody coming up the stairs. So what are you doing, standing there in your pyjamas, in the dark, in the middle of the night, looking for this imaginary assailant?

You turn quickly to the survivor. But at that moment, she looks like a frightened child. At that moment she's reliving some horrible moment from her past, perhaps an unwanted visit in the night from a stepfather, uncle or friend of the family. It's clear from the expression on her face.

As she slept, her subconscious conjured up images of the past—an ordeal from which she never healed. Now, her mind is acting it out like some strange play. Anybody who has helped a survivor heal knows about the nightmares—endless haunting dreams. Although the memories are in the subconscious, to the survivor they are very real. They manifest themselves as nightmares. The survivor thinks she really sees or hears the assailant. She can describe where he is and what he's wearing.

It seemed there was never a moment's rest while Liz was healing. I don't think we ever had a full night's sleep. Turmoil was always present. She'd wake up three, four, maybe six times a night while she was in the process of healing. The nightmares seemed to come in waves. She'd be relatively calm for a few weeks, then the nightmares would start and not stop. It got really tiring at times. Liz wasn't working so she could sleep in the next day, but I was up early for work each morning and it took its toll on me.

What to Expect

The nightmares are much more prevalent during the initial stages of healing or during a part of the process when the survivor is dealing with a lot of trauma. During the healing process, the survivor spends so many waking hours thinking about the abuse which took place that it overwhelms her—even during her sleeping hours. When the survivor goes to bed, the brain is still working, trying to sort out the day's thoughts. As a survivor sleeps, the thoughts continue. Those thoughts form into dreams. Before you know it, the survivor is dreaming of the abuse. It overwhelms her and she wakes, still convinced the abuse is taking place.

Sometimes Liz would get violent during her nightmares. She'd punch me in the back or yell at me for something I didn't do. It's downright confusing to be wakened this way. You automatically assume you've done something wrong, but all you're guilty of is being the person closest to her while she's having a nightmare.

Occasionally, I'd get so sick and tired of the nightmares that I'd just grab a blanket and go sleep on the couch. I'd get upset. I'd stew about it all night, just as if we'd had a real argument. But it wasn't an argument at all. It was a nightmare and it was something Liz couldn't control. I didn't realize that right away. It took me quite a few nights sleeping on the couch before I figured it out. I'd wake up the next morning still angry at Liz, but she'd wake up remembering nothing of the nightmare.

What About Me?

The nightmares can come without warning. The survivor can go days, even weeks, without a nightmare. Then suddenly, one night it can happen again for no reason. It's not surprising that survivors of childhood sexual abuse have these nightmares. Unlike most people, survivors are most threatened in their own homes. They sometimes feel safer outside in open spaces. That's because, as a child, the home may have been where the abuse took place. A survivor can be deathly afraid if left alone in her own home. She'll spend countless hours going around the house, checking cupboards for noises, seeing that the windows and doors are secure. She'll sit down to watch TV, then get up and start the routine all over again.

The survivors usually have a tough time sleeping at night because their fears haunt their thoughts. As a result, they can get very tired. Liz would often have to take naps during the day because she was so tired. She also felt safer sleeping during the day. I encouraged her to take those naps because she had to recharge her batteries. She needed all her strength to deal with her healing. If she didn't get the sleep she wouldn't have the energy to heal properly.

What to Do

Remember, the survivor has no control over what happens when she's sleeping. Her thoughts can't be controlled then. At night, the survivor is truly on her own. She has no control of her thoughts and her world becomes filled with fear and images of sexual abuse. It's as if the brain is trying to sort out some big jigsaw puzzle but gets the pieces in all the wrong places. These nightmares can be especially disturbing to a supporter—not only because of the sleep you lose, but even more because of the help-lessness and despair you feel watching a loved one suffer so much.

Nightmares may always exist for the survivor, but they'll diminish as she recovers. Eventually she'll be free of the pain, but you'll have to wait patiently for this to happen. It's not an overnight thing.

When the survivor is having a nightmare, the best thing to do is soothe her and let her know that she's really loved and protected by you. That could mean getting out of bed—even if it's two o'clock in the morning—and going through the various motions of checking out a noise.

Sure, it's a pain in the butt—especially when you're sure there's nothing there. But, if you do it for her and assure her nobody is there, she'll feel comforted by the fact you protected her. Then she'll sleep again. If you don't, she'll have to go back to sleep with doubts in her mind. She'll probably end up waking you again with more nightmares later on.

When you're confronted with this situation, don't say things like "You're out of your mind" or "Stop playing games and go back to sleep." Also, don't grab the survivor or physically try to force her to lie down. This will only be seen as an aggressive move on your part and likely she'll resist. Remember, when this is going on she's in a frightened state and it won't do you any good to try to restrain her physically. With Liz, I'd just let her scream, punch her pillow or do anything else she wanted to do during a nightmare as long as she didn't hurt herself. I'd just try to pick the right time to intervene and soothe her.

Although the dreams seem very real to the survivor at the time, don't expect her to remember them in the morning. If she does remember them, she might not want to discuss them, so don't push the issue. There's no use trying to discuss them or make rational sense of them the next day, especially if the survivor doesn't want to talk about it. Sometimes it's best to let sleeping dogs lie.

Keep in mind that the dreams are just something she's going to have to go through. Like many of the stages you've already experienced in the healing process, it's just one more step on the ladder.

So don't lose any sleep over it.

Points to Remember

- Nightmares are common for survivors.
- They will be more prevalent during initial stages of her healing.

What About Me?

- Don't blame her for them.
- Help her through them.
- Nightmares will diminish as the survivor recovers.

Chapter Thirteen
Releasing Rage

It's a phrase you're probably tired of hearing by now.

You know the one. She uses it all the time, it really grates on your nerves, she rams it down your throat when you've been caught doing something that didn't please her. It's that all-too-familiar battle cry, the one that's etched in your memory, the one you can never defend against, the one that leaves you red-faced and angry. But let's repeat it anyway, just for the record.

"You're just like all the other men. You can't be trusted."

Sound familiar?

It always gets the same response from you, right? That old familiar feeling wells up inside you. Your face goes red, your blood starts to pump and your palms start sweating. Before you can say "I'm sorry," you're at the boiling point. You're angry and out of control. The months of frustration, stress and accumulated problems take their toll. You blow. You swear at the survivor and take off somewhere, anywhere.

Anger—it's something that's difficult to control. And once it erupts there's not much you can do about it. But you can stop it before you get to the boiling point. That's where you can win the battle.

Anger is something you'll have to deal with if you're going to get safely and sanely through the healing process with a survivor. It's something that plagues every supporter. It's caused by a mountain of things—the pressure, the fact you have limited control over the situation and because things seem hopeless at times. Every supporter feels it at some point during the healing process, but learning how to control it is the real key to survival.

It's easy to let anger spill out in all the wrong ways in all the wrong places. After all, you're dealing with a lot of things that can make you angry. The wrong ways may be punching things, carrying the anger around with you for days on end and venting it on innocent bystanders, friends or co-workers.

Two Types of Anger

As a supporter, you've got two types of anger to deal with— your own anger and that of the survivor.

It's easy to see why the survivor is angry. After all, she has a lot of good reasons to be angry. She was stripped of her innocence as a child; she was abused and was never given a chance at a normal childhood. Because she was a child and wasn't able to handle all the emotions that came with the abuse, the survivor never appropriately dealt with that anger. So it went deep inside her, where it has remained for years. Churned around inside her, it has affected her emotional development. She wasn't able to enjoy life in the same way as other people.

Only now, as the survivor goes through the healing process, is that anger getting a chance to surface. It's being freed up. And when it does come out, watch out. It can come out in a torrent. It can come out in an uncontrollable rage.

Sometimes Liz would just erupt. It could be something very insignificant. It could be something you'd never think would get her upset. But it would set her off. She couldn't help it; the rage would just boil up inside her. It could be the way I looked at her or the way I didn't look at her; it just didn't matter. Sometimes anything could tick her off. It was like there was a little demon inside her, screaming to get out. At times it completely controlled her.

Her Anger

There isn't much you can do once the survivor has crossed that threshold into her world of anger—except give her the time and space she needs to cool off. The anger can erupt at any time because the survivor has so many feelings buried deep inside her. She may not even know they're there. In the early stages of her healing, she won't know when it's coming or what triggers the rage.

Once she starts counseling and dealing with the abuse of her past, the anger is stirred and it has to come out in order for her to heal. As the anger leaves her, though, it will be replaced by good experiences. It's a little like reprogramming a robot. You're taking the bad out and putting the good in. So, even though it may not seem that way, when the anger does come out of her it's a good sign. It's a sign that she's healing. It's a sign that she's on the road to recovery.

The survivor should be encouraged to express her anger—not at you but in a way that is more constructive and positive. She should be encouraged to get the anger out, either through counseling, through hitting a punch bag or teddy bear, or in whatever safe means is possible.

There's little you can do to protect her from the anger she will feel. About all you can do is make sure she isn't abusing herself, you or others while she's getting rid of the anger deep inside of her. Don't take it personally if she directs the anger at you. It's a very difficult thing to stand and take her anger, but keep in mind you're not really the culprit here—just someone who is an easy target. The survivor probably just needs someone to vent her frustrations on and you're the closest thing she's got.

When she's quiet and not going through an anger period, that's a good time to sit with her and talk to her about more constructive ways of letting out her frustrations. Let her know how you feel when she takes her anger out on you. Tell her you'd prefer her to find another, more positive alternative. If she is having an anger session, give her plenty of space to get her anger out. You're not going to prevent it from happening. Just make sure she doesn't harm herself. Make sure, if you can, that she doesn't go driving a car when she's angry. She won't have all her wits about her and could run into trouble.

One time, when Liz was in a state of anger, she hopped in the car and took off. I didn't like it one bit but there wasn't much I could do about it. There was no way of stopping her. A police officer did stop her, however, and gave her a very expensive speeding ticket. The officer also told Liz she'd gone through a stop sign. Liz hadn't even seen the sign. She was lucky. If someone had been coming the other way, the result could have been tragic. When she got home we talked about what happened and she promised that she wouldn't take off in the car again if she had an anger fit.

Your Anger

Getting the anger out is good for the survivor. She has to mourn her loss of innocence as a child, have the chance to express rage at that loss, then begin to heal by replacing that anger with good.

Your anger, though, is a different story. Your anger may be different for many reasons. You may be angry at different things, different people, different circumstances. As a supporter, you may be angry at friends and family for not understanding the situation. You may be angry at the perpetrator for causing all these problems of yours. You may be angry at yourself for not being able to protect the survivor from things that upset her. You may even be angry at the survivor for the time it is taking her to heal. At times, you might also be angry at the counselor for bringing up the horrid past.

Your anger also needs to be vented in a constructive way or it will boil over inappropriately. Make sure you don't direct the anger at the survivor—especially if you're getting angry because of something that has happened in *your* past. If you find during the healing process that you're getting bothered about something, not having a normal reaction to something, it could be because there are some skeletons in your own closet. If you're angry at the survivor for something you shouldn't be angry at her for, it's probably got something to do with your situation and not hers at all.

This opens up a whole new can of worms. If this happens, seek some professional counseling right away. Remember, you don't want to complicate the survivor's healing any more than you have to. She doesn't have the time to deal with your reasons for being angry, so get help from another source to help you figure out your situation.

It could be something simple, something from your own childhood that is triggered by the healing which the survivor is going through. But it is important that you don't get upset with the survivor because she is opening up wounds from your own past.

Somehow—like the survivor—you have to get rid of that anger in a constructive rather than a destructive way. You'll have to find a way of dealing with the immediate situation, then get a longer-term solution in place.

Releasing Anger

When you release your anger, like the survivor, make sure it is released in an appropriate manner. Release your tension as it builds. Don't hold it inside and let it feed on itself. Don't let it get to the point where you're ready to blow. It's difficult to function under these types of circumstances and it won't do your partner any good either.

The best long-term solution is talking out problems when you are both in a calm state of mind. Don't try it when you are both still angry; it won't help. You should both be in a rational state of mind when you try to solve a problem to your mutual satisfaction.

There is one thing that's a certainty in all of this. Letting anger build inside and control you will only send you off in the wrong direction. It won't benefit you, the survivor or anybody else. Remember, she already has a good reason to be angry. Being angry yourself won't help her, or you.

Sometimes, nothing will work when you're both angry. At those times, it is often best to simply take a break. If something the survivor does or says really annoys you, perhaps the best thing to do is leave the situation for a while. That way you both get the chance to calm down. It also gives you both a chance to think about what was said or done, then get together under more rational circumstances and try to solve the dispute. If that doesn't work, try some exercises like breathing or counting to 10 before you reply. These sound like simple things, but they work, believe me.

The Ground Rules

It's important that you discuss ahead of time what steps you both plan to take when you're angry. It's sort of like setting out the ground rules before the game is played. In the end, nobody will get injured, and hopefully the dispute will get solved in a peaceful manner.

Remember, yelling and screaming at each other won't solve anything. And you'll both feel pretty hurt afterwards about what was said. Sometimes you're simply going to have to bite your lip when it comes to a dispute. Nothing you can say or do will change things, and you'll have to accept that.

The dispute could be for a number of reasons. The survivor may be dealing with something from her past or she may just be testing you to see if you really will stand by her side. Either way, a fight will not resolve the problem. And you can bet talking it out won't work at this point. So you'd better work on finding another way to get that anger out of you. That's when you might want to hop in the car, turn on the stereo full blast and yell at the top of your lungs, or take a long drive in the country. Long walks are an especially good way of releasing frustrations.

You might find all this a bit strange at first, but it sure beats holding the anger inside. And, best of all, nobody gets hurt. If you hold it in, the stress and tension will build and it will be sure to erupt in a detrimental way.

I found exercising was a surefire way to release anger. It helped when I went out and worked up a good sweat. Getting the adrenalin flowing was a good way to work things out in my own mind. I was into martial arts and jogging, so when things got tough I always had an outlet. I'd jog for miles. It gave me a chance to sort out my thoughts and put things in perspective, all the while getting some exercise.

It doesn't always have to be exercising, however. There are a number of other ways to get the anger out. You might try something as simple as punching out your pillow, mattress or anything else that's soft. Make sure it is soft, though. You don't want to end up going to the hospital with a broken hand. You might also have a tough time explaining that one to the boss at work.

Yes, at first all this might seem a bit silly. Taking out anger on teddy bears and such is the type of thing you see the crazy people doing in movies. But don't forget, you and the survivor are in a real situation dealing with real anger. She has a right to be angry about what happened to her. You have a right to be angry, too.

So get your anger out in an appropriate way. It'll help your sanity.

Points to Remember

- You both have a right to be angry.
- You need to rid yourselves of that anger in an appropriate way.
- Don't let anger build—try exercising or punching a pillow.
- Decide how you'll deal with anger before it erupts.

Chapter Fourteen
How to Cope

Coping with the pain and trauma of helping a survivor heal from childhood sexual abuse can, in no uncertain terms, be a real pain in the butt. This chapter will draw together many of the things we have already said about what to expect and how to cope.

It is by no means an easy task and it will take all the resources you have. Apart from the pressures of the healing process, there are the pressures that others—your friends, family and co-workers—will put on you.

You'll have to be prepared for the unknown. At times you'll feel like you're walking on eggshells, with no idea what to say or do. If you say the wrong thing, it's like setting off a volcano. Even keeping quiet at the wrong times can prove fatal.

People who help survivors through the healing process are put through the grinder themselves. You'll experience an array of emotions along with the survivor. You'll have to go through the gut-wrenching experience of watching the survivor deal with her torturous past. You'll have to watch her explore the unknown. You'll have to watch her suffer greatly.

Hopefully, you'll stick around long enough to see some of the results of all this. Before that ever comes about, though, you're going to have a real roller-coaster ride which will probably last years. That's right, years. Things can't be worked out overnight. It takes time—a lot of time—to heal.

So, if you've chosen to go on this journey with the survivor, you're going to have to learn how to cope with what's ahead. At times, you'll be tested to the limits. At times, you'll be overwhelmed by it all. At times, you're going to feel like the abuse never goes away. The array of problems and emotions you'll have to cope with are staggering, to say the least. Coping isn't easy; nobody said it was. But you can do it.

Be Tolerant

You have to understand that there are vast numbers of people out there who just don't understand what this is all about. Whether you like it or not, there are still a lot of people who don't know child sexual abuse does occur.

As a result, misconceptions abound. Some will say the survivor put herself in a position to be abused or didn't mind being abused. They'll suggest that she caused the abuse or that she should just forget about it.

If these people knew more about the subject, they probably wouldn't say those things. If they knew more about the devastation it causes in human lives, they probably wouldn't brush it off so easily. Explain your situation to people who are really worth explaining it to, but don't worry about the others. Not everybody deserves an explanation of what you're up to. Apart from family and close friends, it's up to you to decide who you want to tell. You don't want people gossiping behind your back, so use some judgment here.

Release Your Frustrations

Frustration and tension will mount as you help a survivor through the healing process, so it's important to release them early.

Don't let the feelings build too long. Otherwise, they'll erupt all at once—likely in an inappropriate manner. If you allow the anger and frustration to build, it will eventually become a bigger problem—and the survivor may end up as the focus of your anger.

Learn to accept that you're in a tumultuous period in your life and that you have to take time out to release the built-up anger. Understanding your position and accepting that some things are just beyond your control can prove a real asset. It can save you a lot of headaches, sleepless nights and problems with the survivor.

Argue Fairly

Arguments are inevitable during the healing process; there's no doubt about it. They happen even in a normal relationship. Two people can't always agree on everything, right? Add to that the stress and suffering that's involved during healing from child-hood sexual abuse, and you've got a very volatile situation.

When the survivor is healing from abuse, of course, a lot of turmoil exists. She's probably discovering feelings and thoughts she didn't even know existed. So, at times, things are going to get a little tense.

The important thing is to be fair when you argue. Don't hit below the belt. Don't say things that are meant purely to insult the survivor. On the other hand, she also has to be fair with you. It's difficult when tempers are hot, but when you're arguing with the survivor, make sure you keep to the argument. In other words, don't start insulting the survivor's entire family or the way she looks. If you disagree about a point, argue that point, but don't take it beyond that.

It is, perhaps, best to talk about the subject of arguments when you are both calm. It's good to set the ground rules when you're both at ease and you both realize you're doing it for the good of the relationship and for each other. There's no use trying to set the ground rules once you're arguing; it just doesn't work. You're both too worried about finding ways to hurt the other person.

Don't Become a Victim

You have to be careful in all of this that you don't become the victim of abuse yourself.

That doesn't necessarily mean physical abuse. It can be emotional, too. Don't let the survivor use her past to control you and make you do everything she wants you to do. You have to be very careful of this.

If she thinks she can control you by throwing a tantrum, she may do it. If she thinks she can get everything she wants by erupting in a fit of rage, she may do it. So avoid it at all costs. At times, you'll just have to stand your ground. It's easy for the survivor to slip into a power play mode—to attempt to use her past to control you and get everything her own way.

In the end, it can harm both of you. If you're being emotionally abused by the survivor, do your best to put a stop to it.

Set Priorities

This helps you understand what's important in your life.

As you get further into the healing process it's important that you set priorities in your life. Sit down and figure out what's important. To help a survivor heal, some things will have to take a back seat—at least for the time being.

Some things you need—like a job, friends and money. But each of these may have to receive less attention in order to free up time for the survivor's healing. You may have to give up a sport or hobby. Sure, it's tough, but if you're going to go through this, you need to be honest with yourself. You're going to need a lot of time to deal with the survivor.

That doesn't mean you should quit your job, ignore your friends and forget about your financial situation. What it does mean, though, is that you may have to put your career aspirations on hold for a while—until things get a little more settled with the survivor. It's no secret that survivors need a lot of time, patience, love and support. You'll have to realize this and set your priorities accordingly.

Quite simply, you'll go nuts if you try to be everything to everyone. So you need to map out what's important and make some sacrifices. You'll need all your time and energy to focus on what's really important here—helping the survivor get through the healing process.

Find Support

There are times when a good friend will be a lifesaver.

A good friend can be one of your greatest assets in the long run—someone to turn to in times of real crisis, someone who is going to keep you on the level when times get really tough and you need help.

But be sure the friend isn't someone who is going to go out and tell everybody else your business. The friend needs to be someone who is going to listen to you and help you get through the tough times.

It's also a good idea to find out if there is a support group for the two of you in the community. It can be a real learning experience to see that others are in the same boat. Not that it makes you feel any better that someone else is having similar problems, but it may help to know that you are not alone with these troubles. Others in the group might be further along in their recovery and, in times of crisis, they can act as a guiding light. Others can also help educate you about the healing process.

Finding a support group for yourself might be more difficult. There isn't a whole lot out there for the supporters. Check with the local hospital or mental health centre. If you can't find one, you might want to consider starting a group of your own. You can advertise in the newspaper, and once you get enough people who are interested, you can set up the group. It might be wise to get a professional counselor involved in the process—just in case questions or issues arise which nobody knows anything about.

A support group is a great place for you to talk about your feelings. You can ask questions, see how other supporters feel and find out how they've handled certain situations. You can be open and honest in a support group because there will be others who have already been through what you are discovering now. Their support can be invaluable to you.

Don't Neglect Yourself

While you may have to give up some things to make time for the survivor's healing process, that doesn't mean you should neglect yourself. It's a fine line, but make sure you don't spend so much time on the survivor and the healing that you forget about some of your own needs.

Only you will know when your needs are not being met. Go by your gut reaction. When you get to that point, don't feel guilty. You have needs that have to be met too. You deserve to be happy and healthy. Life during the healing process doesn't have to be all bad. While the survivor is important and deserves your attention, you also have to devote time to yourself and your health.

Getting into a regular workout routine is a good idea. You need all your energies and resources to help the survivor get through the healing process, so it's also wise for you to be healthy. You can't be on your toes if you've been neglecting yourself. It's important you stay fit. You may also want to keep an eye on your eating habits. Not only will you feel better about yourself, but it will also give you more energy to deal with the survivor's problems.

Take a Break

It's okay to want to get away from the healing process for a while. The survivor will probably feel the same way.

It's important to have fun even though you're going through a traumatic time in your life. Go and see a comedian, go to a hotel with the survivor for the night—anything to get a break from the healing. Just do something occasionally that will get your mind off the process and give it a break.

Don't forget it's okay to laugh. Laughter is a great way to get rid of frustration, anger and feelings of helplessness, and to recharge your batteries.

Set Realistic Goals

You have to accept the limits of what both you and the survivor can do. Don't expect too much of the survivor too fast. She won't be able to run before she can walk. The healing process takes time, so be prepared for that and set your goals accordingly.

If you expect too much of yourself and too much from the survivor, you're only going to put more pressure on yourself. It's a good idea to sit down with the survivor and set your goals. You'll probably want to keep in mind that you'll need a lot of down time—times you can just sit with the survivor and talk things over.

Relax

Lastly, remember that helping someone heal from childhood sexual abuse is like running a marathon. Pacing yourself is very important. No marathon runner tries to go too far, too fast. They don't sprint the entire 26 miles. They pace themselves. They just keep plugging away.

So try and follow their lead. Relax and pace yourself.

What About Me?

Points to Remember

- Be tolerant.
- Release your frustrations.
- Argue fairly.
- Don't become a victim.
- Set priorities.
- Get a good friend or participate in a support group.
- Don't neglect yourself.
- Take breaks.
- Set realistic goals.
- Relax.

Chapter Fifteen
Taking a Break

It takes a lot of time, patience and understanding to help a survivor heal.

The constant pressure and problems associated with healing can tax your reserves to the limit. It can drain you both physically and mentally, and if you're not careful, it can leave you a bundle of nerves.

If you don't schedule some breaks from it all, you're going to buckle under all the pressure—especially down the road as the healing process drags on. If you don't maintain your body as well as your mind you'll only end up a burden to the survivor. You won't be up to helping her when times get tough. You might not have the energy; you might not have the patience; you might not have the willpower.

You need to be physically as well as mentally fit for what's ahead, for whatever comes up on the survivor's road to recovery. To do this you've got to eat properly, exercise and, above all, take regular breaks from the healing process. It's very important to take breaks.

In a way, your body is like a car engine. It needs to be maintained. You wouldn't expect your car to keep running forever without an oil change or proper maintenance, would you? The same goes for your body. While you're helping someone heal from the trauma of childhood sexual abuse, your body is under a tremendous amount of stress and pressure. It needs time to recuperate and recharge.

Think of yourself as a professional athlete. You don't see a professional athlete compete all year round without rest. You don't see them compete when they are injured. That's because they realize they need to take breaks, they need time to heal in order to do a better job when they compete again. So, just like the athlete, both you and the survivor need time away from the healing process. That way, when you get back to the task at hand, you're in better shape to deal with things. You'll have more energy, more patience and a fresher outlook. You won't be as tired. You'll have had time to put things in perspective, think things over in a non-stressful environment, away from the heat of the action.

Yes, a lot of your time will be devoted to helping the survivor heal. But there are other things that are important in life too, and you need to take some time to enjoy these things. You have to schedule some time to do things that you and the survivor really enjoy doing together. If you don't, it will only add to the problems.

Liz and I used to go fishing in order to get a break. It was relaxing and stress-free, and we could be in our own little worlds yet still spend time together. It was a great way to unwind and give ourselves a rest from the rigors of healing. After a day fishing, we'd return home relaxed and ready to face the world again. It wasn't so much the fishing that helped. It was just getting away to a place where there weren't any stresses. It gave our bodies time to recover.

She'll Enjoy It Too

You'll probably find out that the survivor enjoys breaks from the healing just as much as you do. After all, she can get physically and mentally exhausted by the whole process as well, perhaps even more than you. She'll get through things a lot easier if she tries to heal a little bit at a time with breaks in between, rather than tackling everything at once. It can overwhelm her if she doesn't get a break.

The survivor has to make the decision to take the break—you can't do it for her—but she'll likely find that she needs some time away in order to reflect on the healing she's done, in order to see how far she's come. It can be frustrating for the survivor to keep pushing forward without reflecting on how much she's accomplished. She needs to know she's progressing. In the long run, it will give her more strength and courage to continue.

Sometimes it can be tough scheduling a break away from the action. But it doesn't have to be for a long period of time. It could be a weekend at the cottage or a day at the beach—as long as it's some quality time away from the healing.

If it's not possible to get away for a long period of time, don't worry. Just do what you can. Do your best to schedule some events or activities that will give you some time away. It could be anything from skiing in the winter to swimming in the summer. Perhaps a night at the movies, a day golfing or watching a sports event might help to take off some of the pressure. Go see a comedy show. That can be a great relief. So can a brisk walk, in the winter or summer. It's amazing the things that can take your mind off the healing for a while.

The important thing to remember here is that you should, at times, do something—anything—that takes your mind off the healing. It takes a long time for a survivor to heal from abuse, and that sort of constant tension puts a lot of stress on the body. Over time, that stress will take its toll unless you do something to stop it.

I remember how the constant talk of abuse used to drive me crazy. It just seemed to go on and on; Liz wouldn't stop talking about it. We talked about the abuse every day. Sometimes I felt like walking out the door and taking a few days off. All my waking hours seemed to be spent talking about it. After a while, I talked to Liz and found out she felt the same way, so we decided to do something about it. We started to schedule time off from the healing. It gave us something to look forward to and we both felt better knowing that we were going to have some quality time together.

Don't Feel Guilty

Don't feel guilty about taking some time off from the healing process. It takes a long time for the survivor to heal, and both you and the survivor have to maintain some semblance of an enjoyable life during the healing. You are allowed to have a life during the healing process, and it's better that you do. You've got to find a balance.

What About Me?

There will be many times when the survivor is totally involved in her healing. But there also will be times when she isn't dealing with it at all. When you find the survivor is getting to the point of needing that break, help her arrange one. Likewise, when you find yourself in dire need of a break, make sure you take one. There is one word of warning in all of this, though. When you're on one of those breaks, don't get too caught up in everything and forget that the survivor still has more healing to do. It can be downright frustrating to spend a great weekend at the cottage, only to find the survivor facing her problems again on Monday morning. You have to be prepared for that to happen because it does.

I used to make the mistake of thinking everything was turning around after a great weekend or outing away from the healing process. But the bubble would always burst and we'd soon be right back into the thick of healing again. At first it was disappointing because I didn't realize how much time it takes for a survivor to heal. But when it started to happen over and over again, I began to realize it was going to take time—a lot of time. Eventually, I accepted that we could have great times away from the healing, but that Liz, at some point, had to get back to the job at hand.

Although you're entitled to have a good time when you're on a break, remember the survivor still has to return to her healing. Just because she's had some time off doesn't mean everything is peachy again. It won't be, and you should be cognizant of that. If you're not, you could be in for some disappointments.

As you go through the healing process, you'll probably find that you fall into a routine of intense healing followed by periods of good time. As the survivor begins to heal more, the good times will last a little longer. Eventually, there will be more good times than bad.

However, it's wise to remember that, like a car motor, the survivor can't go full throttle all the time. And neither can you. So make sure the two of you schedule the time for rest and relaxation. That way you'll both get through this without running out of gas.

Points to Remember

- It takes a lot of time for a survivor to heal.
- Both you and the survivor need breaks from the healing process.
- Don't feel guilty about taking time off.
- After a break, the survivor still has to get back to the job of healing.

Chapter Sixteen
Sexual Relations

Remember when you were a kid? Remember when you were in the candy store and wanted some sweets but couldn't have them?

Well, guys, sorry to be the bearer of bad news, but it can be pretty much the same with sex. When you want to have sex with someone who is healing from childhood sexual abuse, you will sometimes feel like that kid in the candy store again. It may be something you really want, but you just can't have. That's the reality of the situation and you're going to have to accept it—the sooner the better.

Problems with sex can surface any time. They can start when you approach the survivor. She may shy away and want nothing to do with you. It can happen when you're already involved in the act. Suddenly she may ask you to stop. It can happen right after the act. She may roll over and go quiet, not wanting you to be close to her.

Whatever the case, these refusals can be the most difficult, the most awkward situations you'll have to deal with as you help a survivor heal from abuse. Sex can stir up a lot of emotions and feelings.

To some men, even the temporary loss of sexual relations can cause a lot of problems. The thought of losing your sex life with the survivor shakes the very roots of your survival. It's probably one of the things you were most frightened of when the survivor started the healing process. It may have been the first thing people warned you about when they heard your wife was healing from childhood sexual abuse. It's probably something that weighed on your mind for some time before it actually happened.

It might sound a little selfish, but who can blame you? You've been raised to think that sex is one of the most important things in the world. And for years you've probably enjoyed a fairly normal sex life with your partner—only to have the rug pulled out from under your feet. It's no surprise, then, that when you're refused sex it takes a little time to get used to. Who can blame you for being a bit frazzled? Without sex, you start to question yourself, your world, everything around you. You wonder if you're losing it. You get frustrated and the tension builds. It's normal for sex—or lack of it—to cause a lot of problems in relationships in which a survivor is healing from abuse. Sometimes it can even cause breakups.

I remember how frustrated I got during the healing process. Liz and I had such a great sex life before she started healing from the abuse. We never had a problem, but after she started healing it became a big problem for us. Sometimes we'd be getting in the mood, then suddenly she'd go cold for no reason at all. All she would tell me is that she was having bad thoughts. At first, I didn't understand. But later, as I became more familiar with what she was going through, I learned it wasn't me and it wasn't us that were the problem. It was the abuse of her past that was causing our difficulties.

After a while, I learned just to deal with it by taking a long, cold shower. Believe me, I took a lot of long, cold showers in those days.

Why Sex Is So Important

Sex means a lot to most guys. No doubt about it. The reason for all this is simple. It's in your genes. Let me explain. You see, males and females differ in both appearance and behavior, just because of those little sex hormones that are inside you. It's the androgens, estrogens and progestins that determine your sexuality. You don't control them. They control you. They're like little chemical messengers in the body and they affect the body processes, the body developments and the behaviors of men and women.

Recent studies of animals have shown that not only do the sexual hormones directly influence behavior, but they also control certain aspects of behavior by organizing the structure of the brain early in life. So, whether you like it or not, you have them. And they're there to stay. There's nothing you can do about it.

The hormones are the reason you act and feel differently from a woman. It's a fact that's been recognized for centuries. Even primitive societies recognized the fact that tissue from the male testes contained substances that affected body appearance and behavior. These substances are the male hormones called androgens. The main type of androgen is called testosterone.

The ancient Chinese alchemists gave portions of testes as medical treatment to improve sexual ability. The ancient Greeks learned that the castration of bulls—removing their testes—improved both the temperament of the animal and the meat. Chicken farmers have long known that the castration of a cock will produce a plump, juicy capon.

Likewise, we know that in humans, removing the sexual hormones before adulthood will prevent the development of adult sexual characteristics. In 18th-century Europe, young boys were castrated to keep their voices high and beautiful.

Studies have shown that increased androgen levels—which exist in the male and not the female—are clearly linked to more aggressive behavior. Now, this isn't to suggest such drastic measures as castration or pills to control your androgen levels and help you get through periods without sex. But you'll have to find another, perhaps less painful way of controlling yourself.

It is important, however, that you're aware of the fact you are physically different from the survivor and there are reasons you get so hung up on sex. That's why it can cause so many problems and frustrations when you can't have what you want.

Sex Does Exist

Sex can exist during the healing process, albeit on a more sporadic basis than you were probably used to before the survivor started healing. At times sex won't be a problem at all. But, as sure as the sun rises and sets, as sure as the world is round, as sure as there are pyramids in Egypt, there are going to be times when sexual relations will just be non-existent in your relationship with the survivor. No matter how hard you try, your advances will be refused by the survivor. At times during the healing process, sex is just out of the question.

During these times, you're going to feel like that kid in the candy store again—wanting but not getting. But it's best not to push the issue. How you feel about this situation will be much different from the way the survivor feels, and what you and the survivor think about sex at the time are probably also two different things. To you, sex may be a gratifying and satisfying act of love between two caring people. To the survivor, though, sexual acts can stir up much different feelings.

I saw it in Liz many times. One minute she'd be interested in having sex, the next, it would be the last thing on her mind. I'd get so frustrated because it would all be so confusing. She'd tell me she was looking forward to spending time alone with me and then, when we were finally alone, she'd back off. She wouldn't be at all interested. Other times, we'd have sex, then she'd want nothing to do with me afterwards. Again, it wasn't me that was the problem. It was the abuse. Because the abuse was of a sexual nature, it's easy to understand why a survivor has so much trouble in adult life separating sex on consent—that which occurs between two adults who are in love—and the type that occurs between a perpetrator and an abused child. As the survivor heals, she'll begin to differentiate.

You can't blame the survivor for feeling this way. It's only natural that a survivor sometimes gets confused when you touch her. She's got a lot to figure out. What is good touching? What is bad touching? What feels good? What doesn't? What is right? What is wrong? As a young child, the survivor was forced or manipulated into having sex. As an adult, she needs time to realize she has a choice in the matter. It can cause a lot of tension and you might get tired of all the refusals you get. But you'll just have to persevere until things get better. In the end, the survivor will figure things out. But it's going to take some time.

For you, going without sex is a big deal. After all, you're not healing from abuse and those little androgens can drive you crazy. It can be really tough when you're going nowhere fast.

What About Me?

Bite Your Lip

When sex obviously isn't in the cards, it's best just to bite your lip and zip your zip. Chasing the survivor all over the house, looking for affection in all the wrong places, won't help a bit. Things will only get worse. And you can be sure you won't get any sex out of the deal.

The best remedy is just to leave her alone. If she doesn't want it, don't attempt it. When the child abuse survivor makes it clear she's not in the mood, listen to her. She may be dealing with something she can't explain very well to you. She may be dealing with something she doesn't want to explain to you. It might be something you won't understand. It might be something you won't want to understand. It might be something she doesn't want to talk about quite yet. In any event, keep your hands to yourself—unless the survivor asks. Trying to have sex with a survivor who doesn't really want it is plainly abuse in itself.

Having said all of this, it doesn't mean you shouldn't have feelings of your own about the issue. It's completely normal for you to feel frustrated by the lack of sex. After all, think of how you've been conditioned to think by our society. Almost every movie you watch shows a studly guy getting what he wants from a woman—sex, sex and more sex, whenever the guy wants it. It's the James Bond scenario. He snaps his fingers and the girl appears, reading and willing. So, if we follow this method of thinking, a guy who can't get sex is a wimp, right? It's no wonder you feel ashamed, unattractive, less of a man when you get refused sex. Not to mention the frustration.

Forget all that, though. It's only the movies. And those people are just actors. The important thing to remember is that none of this is personal, so don't take it to heart. It's not your fault you're not getting sex, and it's not hers. It's just one of those things.

If the survivor doesn't want sex, it's not because you've failed as a man and it's not because you don't please her. It's not because you're not a good lover. It's not because there's somebody else. You could be Robert Redford and the survivor still wouldn't have an interest in sex. You could wear your sexiest clothes, your best aftershave, and serve up the best wine; none of it would matter. When she doesn't have an interest, she doesn't have an interest, and nothing you say or do will change that. The problem is the abuse. That's what's really stopping the survivor from having sex.

It's Your Problem

If you're having real problems dealing with all this—and find you really have to relieve yourself in some way—remember that's your problem to solve. It's not hers. You're going to have to find another way of relieving those built-up desires. We won't get into how to do that. Suffice it to say that masturbation, exercise and yelling in the car are all ways of getting rid of frustrations. How you relieve your sexual tensions is a personal matter. You probably managed it as a teenager, so you can probably figure out a way now.

If you're having a really tough time with all of this, it's best to seek professional help. It's your choice, but remember, at this stage in the game, the survivor doesn't need to feel pressured because you have built-up frustrations. She has other, more pressing things on her mind and she needs all her energies and resources to deal with that.

Putting additional pressure on her because of sex won't do either of you any good. Approaching her over and over again about sex isn't going to help the problem. It probably will make things worse.

If it's been a while and you're both lying in bed at night, don't say things like "Is tonight the night?" or "How long do I have to wait?" You might as well forget even asking, and just grab a blanket and head for the couch. You can be sure the question won't get a positive response.

Remember, you have to consider the feelings of the survivor. Your feelings aren't the important thing here; you'll have to work them out elsewhere. Talking to a friend or counselor might help you. The survivor needs her own time to sort things out. If you try to push her, she'll only resist. She's working through a lot of feelings and emotions as she tries to heal, and presenting her with your problems won't help at all.

To figure out how she feels, think of how you felt after someone close to you died. Sounds morbid, but it's a good analogy. Remember how it affected you? Remember how empty you felt inside? Sex was probably the last thing on your mind. That will give you some idea of how the survivor feels, and the kind of consideration you need to show for her feelings.

Keep in mind that she could be grieving the loss of her past or the loss of her childhood. But, if you keep bugging her about sex, you're definitely pushing the wrong buttons. You're simply going to have to play the waiting game. And that doesn't mean repeatedly asking her "Is today the day?" If you're hovering around her like a vulture, you can be sure she will feel pressured by that and it won't speed things up at all.

A Union Is More Than Sex

Don't forget that a union between two people is based on more than sex. Maybe it's a good time, when sex is non-existent, to work on the other areas of your relationship. Sometimes the survivor will just want to hug and talk. She may want to be touched, but not have sex. Other times she will want to have normal sexual relations with you.

Which brings up another very important point. If you do have sex with the survivor, make sure you never abuse her. That means no vulgar language, slapping or any other means of control. And don't ever ask her to do something she doesn't really enjoy doing. The worst thing you can do when having sex is to remind her of the abuse.

It is, on the other hand, important for the survivor to make her intentions clear to you. If she just wants to be hugged, she should tell you that when she approaches you. If she just wants to talk, she should let you know that too. It avoids any confusion. That way you don't mistake a hug for a sexual gesture. It makes it easier if you know what's going on because you won't cross the boundary.

Liz and I worked out a plan that was very simple. She'd tell me in no uncertain terms whether she was interested in sex or not. I still had to deal with the pent-up frustration, but it helped solve a lot of difficulties and I think in the end it helped her heal more quickly knowing that I cared about her well-being. She didn't have the worry of playing a guessing game with me. If she was interested in sex, I knew it. If she wasn't interested in sex, I knew that as well. At least there was no confusion about the issue.

You'll need open lines of communication to get through this stage in the process. The key to this part of the puzzle is to talk things out, discuss how you both feel about the situation. Be honest with each other here. The survivor has to make her intentions known and the supporter has to know his limits.

If you're wondering about sex with the survivor, ask her. She'll be glad you did. Remember, she still loves you and it's difficult sometimes to push you away. Ask her, though, when you are both calm and not engaging in sexual contact. It's good to have the ground rules set up before anything happens.

I found the best way to iron out any potential problems with sex was to let the survivor initiate any sexual contact. I left it solely up to Liz whether she wanted to have sex or not. That way I wasn't constantly badgering her when she wasn't in the mood. And when she *was* in the mood, I knew.

By now, it probably seems clear that you have to do a lot of giving and be very understanding while the survivor deals with her past. Well, that's exactly what it boils down to. But it can be done. Remember, you're doing it for the betterment of your relationship. Relationships are not always perfectly balanced; sometimes one person has to give more than the other. During the healing process, you're doing most of the giving. Perhaps the favor will be returned, once the survivor has healed and your relationship continues.

It's a very touchy situation, and the rules about sex can't be set in stone. But, when things get rough, rest assured there is a saving grace in all of this. Sometime, somehow—when you're least expecting it—the survivor will lock her arms around you and look at you with those bedroom eyes. Yes, guys, the sex will return. And when it does, all that waiting and suffering won't matter one bit. Even if you're not prepared, it's a guarantee you'll be ready for it.

Points to Remember

- The chemicals inside men and women make them different.
- Sex can exist during the healing process.
- Don't have sex with the survivor if she doesn't want to.
- It's not your fault she's not interested.
- Relieving your sexual frustrations is your own problem.
- A healthy union between two people is more than sex.
- Have open lines of communication about sex.

Chapter Seventeen
Is It Worth It?

It's probably crossed your mind by now. In fact, you've probably spent countless hours and many sleepless nights thinking about it. It's the million-dollar question—the one you've probably been trying to figure out since you started helping the survivor heal.

Is it worth it? Is there an end to all this seemingly endless pain and suffering? And how long will it all take? How can you tell when a survivor has healed?

Well, glad you've asked. For starters, it's quite normal to think about these things. Few supporters go through the process without wondering the same thing. After all, who wants to put up with all this turmoil and anguish if there's no light at the end of the tunnel? Only a crazy man would do it, right? Certainly no one in their right mind.

Before I answer that all-important question, though, there are a few very important things you should know about the healing process.

First, it's important to remember that recovery is a very lengthy process. You can't rush the survivor through her healing. She's controlled by an inner clock. She can't just suddenly take all those mixed-up emotions and feelings inside her and wipe them out in a single blow. It would be great if she could, but we know it's simply not possible. The survivor must work slowly and methodically through her feelings.

It's something like a good doctor. He doesn't rush you into surgery when he thinks something is seriously wrong; he does tests to confirm his suspicions before he starts an operation. The survivor, too, has to go one step at a time. She needs to perform tests, find out the results and decide on the next step.

The survivor needs time to sort out her feelings. She needs time to work out what is right and wrong. She needs time to separate good from bad. Don't forget, she's carried these pent-up frustrations and feelings inside her for years. It's going to take time to get them out in a good way. If she goes too fast, she'll end up missing something, then have to go back again to catch up.

It Doesn't Happen Overnight

Healing from childhood sexual abuse is much like grieving a death. It takes time—a different amount of time for each individual—and you can't be rushed. You have to go through the different stages of recovery, and feel the full effects of each stage, before you are over the pain of the death. You have to get the feelings out and deal with them before you can move on to the next stage. If a step is missed in the grieving process, the person will have to take time out later on to go back and pick up the pieces of the puzzle.

The length of time it takes someone to heal can vary. It depends so much on the circumstances of abuse, how deeply it affects the survivor, what type of person the survivor is and how she copes. It also depends on such things as her supports, how much time she has to devote to the healing process and how badly she wants to heal.

There are a number of variables at work here, so it's impossible to say exactly how long someone should take to heal. Someone who has good supports, a lot of time to devote to healing and has a real desire to change the way she thinks and feels about life should heal more quickly. Someone who, for example, has children of her own to take care of and a job to keep up might take longer because she has other commitments and can't spend as much time dealing with the healing process.

There's no sure-fire formula to tell how long it can take someone to heal. We're all different. Some people just naturally take longer than others. It's a safe bet, however, the survivor will need many months and, more likely, years to heal. Yes, it may sound like a long time, but it can't be rushed.

It would be miraculous, to say the least, if it took only a matter of weeks for a survivor to undo what was years in the making and what was then bottled up for many years afterwards. By now, though—having read the previous chapters of this book—you realize how many stages the survivor must go through in order to heal.

Don't Get Stuck in a Rut

One thing that can really drag out the process is when the survivor gets stuck in one of the stages of recovery. Usually it's the suffering stage. Rather than moving forward and achieving a resolution, she gets into a position where she seems to be spinning her wheels, going nowhere fast. Sometimes, for a number of reasons, the survivor just can't seem to move on. She might end up blocking the entire unpleasant past out of her mind for months or even years. It happens because this is one of the ways the mind protects itself from pain, but it also prevents the victim from progressing.

Sometimes the survivor can't work things out to her own satisfaction. She may end up blaming herself for what happened to her. This is where she may need a gentle push from you in the right direction. If you see this happening to the survivor, suggest she seek help from a professional counselor so that she'll get back on track.

All this takes time, but it really isn't as bad as it sounds. You're going to have to deal with a lot of problems caused by the abuse, but you can still have a lot of good times too. Don't think you have to sit around waiting for the whole thing to end. It isn't all work and no play.

Although it's difficult, try not to keep track of the time it takes the survivor to heal. Somewhere in the back of your mind you're going to have a little clock running that remembers when the whole process started, but try not to keep harping the survivor about it.

For example, don't say things like "Geez, dear. How long is all this stuff going to take? You've been at this healing thing for a year now. When is it ever going to end?"

Sure, you have a right to feel a bit frustrated by the whole thing, but don't bug her about it. It's not her fault. If she feels you're keeping track of the time, it's only going to slow down the whole process. The survivor is likely going to feel more pressure and buck the whole healing thing. And that won't do either of you any good. So remember, give her time—all the time she needs. Healing is a lot like climbing a very long ladder, and the survivor has to take one step at a time. She has to make sure she doesn't miss any steps on the way up.

Recovery

Once the survivor is well on her way to recovery—when she has got a lot of the anger and other feelings out of her—you won't need someone to tell you. You'll notice it right way. Like a child, the survivor will begin to thirst for some of the things she missed out on when she was young. It could be something like schooling. Many survivors of childhood sexual abuse do poorly at school or drop out because their mind was elsewhere and wasn't on their schoolwork.

As the survivor reaches the end of her healing process, she'll want to start making up for lost time. She may want to do things like go for more education, read books and learn new skills. She may start taking more of an interest in the world around her. She'll have better success at all this now because her mind is less cluttered and she'll be able to take more in.

Her ambitions will rise too. Instead of settling for second best, she may want to set more lofty goals—a better job, house, or future. It's like watching a flower bloom, like watching a child grow into adulthood—but a lot more quickly. The mind that was once cluttered and confused becomes more clear and concise.

You'll probably get a real kick out of all this because it will probably be the first really clear indication you have that the survivor is healing. Before, the only way you could judge was if she was getting her anger out. And that wasn't much fun to go through. But now, the process looks more positive. So take time and enjoy it.

You'll see genuine happiness in the survivor's face as she moves ahead on the road to recovery. The change will be noticeable and remarkable at the same time. It can also be a little scary for the supporter, though. Suddenly the person that you've been used to is showing signs of change. Although it's change for the better, it could make you feel a bit uneasy. You may feel you're losing touch with her as she sets out on her quest for knowledge. This is quite natural. She is changing, but rest assured she's still the same person. It's just that she doesn't have all that rotten stuff inside her any more. What you're going to be left with is the good stuff you liked about the survivor in the first place.

Your attitude can be important here. Instead of feeling uneasy about the changes she's going through, get involved in the whole process. If you don't, you could be left behind. At this stage, the survivor wants to take more control over her life and head in a positive direction. Somehow, you should find a way to fit into her plans.

The survivor will probably want to change a lot of things about herself. It could be her job, her career, where she lives, anything that can be changed. So don't buck it. This whole thing could be good for you too. Over the years, you may have become too set in your ways. Sometimes change is exactly what you need to get kick started. Helping the survivor in her quest for new knowledge could be a lot of fun for you too.

Setbacks Happen

Although things may be going well, be prepared for the occasional setback. The survivor may heal, but she is never completely free from her past. Eventually she will leave behind the pain and will no longer mourn for a lost childhood, but she will always remember what happened to her. This is something that she—and you—will just have to live with. You can't get someone to forget their past. The best you can hope for is that she won't suffer any more because of it.

The past will always exist for her, somewhere in the crevices of her mind. When she's healed, though, she'll have put the past in perspective and have the ability to prevent it from interfering in her present life. The past will have become bearable and it will have been put in its rightful place—the past.

What About Me?

But, having said all this, let's get back to the original question: "Is it worth it?" Well, if you ask a supporter who is just starting the process, the answer might not be too positive. That's because he doesn't understand many things and doesn't know if it will end. But if you ask someone who has been through the process—someone who is at the end of helping a survivor heal—you'll get an easy answer.

They've watched the survivor change for the better. They've got a stronger relationship. They've got a better future. For those who've gone through the whole process the answer is quite simple. It's an unequivocal *yes*.

Points to Remember

- The survivor has to work slowly through the healing process.
- Survivors heal at different rates, depending on a number of things.
- Help the survivor make sure she doesn't get stuck in the suffering stage.
- You'll know when the survivor has healed.
- It *is* worth it.

Acknowledgments

I am indebted to a number of people for making this book possible.

I would like to thank Creative Bound publisher Gail Pike for believing in this book.

My editor Janet Shorten deserves an award for her insightful guidance.

Groups helpful in providing information for this book include:
- The National Clearinghouse on Family Violence
- The Ontario Women's Directorate
- The Metropolitan Toronto Special Committee on Child Abuse.

Other good books on this subject include:
Allies in Healing by Ellen Bass and Laura Davis (1991) New York: Harper and Row
Partners in Recovery by Beverly Engel (1991) New York: Fawcett Columbine

Individuals or groups wishing to order additional copies of this book, may do so by contacting the publisher:

Creative Bound Inc.
P.O. Box 424
Carp, Ontario, Canada K0A 1L0
TEL: (613) 831-3641
FAX: (613) 831-3643